MY FRENCH PLATTER
REPLENISHED

In Search of a Dream Life in France

ANNEMARIE RAWSON

Contents

RECIPES

1

A Fresh Start

'Look at you both! I can't believe the change in you.' Siobhan stepped back to take us in properly then rushed forward, putting her arms around us and kissing us on both cheeks. 'Particularly you, Annemarie. You're tanned and glowing and look like a new woman.'

'I feel like it, believe me.' I grinned inanely at her. I almost had to pinch myself to believe how different our life was since Steve, my husband, and I left our home in New Zealand to embark on our first employment in France, an experience I shared in *My French Platter*. We'd moved 12,000 miles across the world to work as estate managers for London art gallery owners Tristan and Richard at Mas de Lavande, their second home in Southwest France. The filth we'd encountered and having to rely on dilapidated equipment in a run-down kitchen before our belligerent and contrary boss unceremoniously sacked us had certainly not been on the agenda. My stress levels had gone through the roof working there and I'd lost a little of my joie de vivre, as well as several kilos in weight. It was a difficult time but the glorious French countryside and the people we met had turned it into an incredible experience.

'Don't stand on the doorstep. Come in, come in and tell us all about your Tuscan holiday.' Siobhan grabbed me by the elbow and pulled me inside. 'I'm dying to hear your news. I'll put the kettle on.'

After our exhausting stint at Mas de Lavande, London friends had invited us to spend a week with the family in a Tuscan villa to enjoy some much-needed R&R. The luxurious villa and their company had been just the tonic Steve and I needed to restore ourselves.

Siobhan pushed the front door shut, turned and yelled up the staircase, 'Doug, hurry up and come down. Annemarie and Steve are back from Tuscany. You won't believe it's them. C'mon. I'm making coffee.' Siobhan bustled us through into the kitchen, firing off a hundred questions at the same time.

Siobhan and Doug were the first people we met when we initially arrived in France and we'd become great friends. They were English, with two young children, had lived in France for about eight years and became our lifesavers, taking us in when everything turned nasty and our employer forced us to leave Mas de Lavande with nowhere to go.

As a result of their help, we'd secured two jobs. The first was an interim job with Denise and Ian in Lisle-sur-Tarn at Domaine de Ménerque. In exchange for 30 hours' work a week in their extensive and formal parterre garden, we could live in their cottage across the driveway, rent-free. This would be home until we moved to full-time, paid employment at Combe de Merigot, near Gaillac (pronounced Guy-ak), to work for Mary and Symon, an English couple with a London home but who lived and worked in New York at the time.

Gaillac is a historic wine-producing region located just northeast of Toulouse. It's one of France's oldest viticultural areas, established in Roman times, and still produces a wide variety of wine. It celebrates its diverse wine production at the Fête des Vins every summer during August. This week-long event, held in the magnificent setting of Foucaud Park in the shade of centuries-old trees, is great fun and where you can meet with local winegrowers.

The next day we again met up with Doug and Siobhan and followed them in our car to take another peek at Combe de Merigot. No one was currently at the house and Doug didn't have a key so we would only be able to walk around the property and peer in the windows for now. It was a short but picturesque drive from Gaillac, crossing the D18 and accelerating up the hill. Miniature chandeliers of plump, purple grapes hanging from orderly rows of vines flashed past on our left, and on our right, undulating, sun-browned hills with several farmhouses, a few sparsely dotted trees and grazing sheep came into view.

Enormous, rustic iron gates and imposing pillars topped with stone urns framed the entrance to Combe de Merigot. The house was a sight to behold, blending seamlessly into the landscape. A poplar-tree-lined drive meandered down an incline, crossed a small bridge and came to a stop next to the pale, pink-bricked, three-storeyed house. I can only describe it as majestic. Grapevines climbed the slope at the rear of the house up to a forested ridge, which created a natural fence line for the back perimeter of the property.

A large, shimmering pond with a short jetty sat on one side of the drive. Vibrant, green lily pads floated on the surface and weeping willows lining the far side waltzed in the whispering breeze.

An hour flew by as we took in all that the property offered, including a magnificent pool complex with a summer dining room as well as a towering *pigeonnier* (pigeon loft) at the rear of the house. It sounds fanciful but this house 'spoke' to me, as it had the first time we'd seen it, and I just knew this was the place for us.

Our new working life was about to unfold and we were hoping it would be infinitely better and happier than the previous one.

We had yet to meet Mary and Symon. The employment

arrangements had been completed over Skype and via email but all our dealings with them to date left me feeling positive and very comfortable with our decision.

Gut instinct is everything, or so I hoped…

2

Our Interim Job at Domaine de Ménerque

Domaine de Ménerque started life over a hundred years ago as a winery, having its own vines and *pigeonnier* with the pigeon dung used as fertiliser and the pigeon itself as food for the table. Their wines were known to be exceptional. The stark and very plain, concrete-finished rear of the property sat close to the road and its bare, unshuttered, gloomy windows made it look singularly unappealing. When we walked down the drive at the side of the house, however, we found the most beautiful, imposing frontage which faced the now-extensive garden. A double-balustrade set of steps led up to the front door and each end of the house had square towers with a pyramid-shaped roof finish, giving the impression of turrets. Every window on this side was perfectly aligned and framed with the typical French-blue painted shutters. It was a magnificent-looking house.

The front garden was laid out in a formal, box-hedge/parterre style with gravel pathways, lawn and various trees, including fruit trees and 20 enormous palms. A pond, filled with water lilies and goldfish, was set right in the middle of the parterre with a tinkling water feature adding a little music. The property hosted two swimming pools—a large one for the main house and a smaller one for the cottage, which sat across the driveway. When the property was still a winery, the cottage was for the workers.

Well and truly modernised now, it was just perfect for us and beautifully clean, with two bedrooms and a bathroom upstairs, and a good-sized kitchen/dining/living area and a loo downstairs. Large French doors gave plenty of light into the living room and opened out onto a terrace with an outdoor table and chairs and a gate in the fence that led to our pool. It was all such luxury after our dreadful accommodation at Mas de Lavande, where the furniture was rickety and furnishings were tatty and worn. It didn't take us long to unpack and settle in, stowing our suitcases in the big cupboard under the stairs. I'd just put the kettle on when there was a knock at the door. It was Denise.

'Settling in OK? D'you fancy popping over for an *apéro* at 5? It's lovely and warm so we could sit in the garden.'

'That would be so nice, thank you. We'll definitely see you at 5.' I smiled at her.

That set the scene. Denise came to us the following day and from then on we would often spend our early evenings together if we were both home. It wasn't long before she was bringing out a mid-morning pot of coffee.

'Coffee's ready, you two,' she'd call, carrying her laden tray down the steps to the outdoor table.

We'd down tools, pull off our gloves and head for the table, where the three of us would sit under the shade of the big, cream, square umbrella and chat. One morning, shortly after we started working there, Denise pushed the plunger down, poured our coffee and passed the cups around.

'Ian's down from Luxembourg this weekend. D'you fancy coming in for supper on Saturday night? You haven't really had the chance to get to know him as you only had a brief chat when you came to look at the place.'

'Oh, nice, yes, we'd love to. Thank you. Can I bring a salad or dessert?' I offered.

'A salad would be super, thanks. I know Ian will want to barbecue some steaks. I'll sort a quick dessert.'

Ian was based in Luxembourg for his work. Over the summer he was back nearly every weekend as well as a week here and there. During winter, Denise would be with him in Luxembourg or the UK visiting family and would come to the French house for shorter periods. The housing market was depressed and Denise and Ian, like other English people in our area, were trying to sell their French home, not only because of the economic situation but also because it was rumoured the French government was looking to bring in a huge tax on foreign-owned homes. Their property had been on the market for two years with no sale in sight. It was demoralising for everyone concerned.

Denise and Ian turned out to be so different to Tristan at Mas de Lavande who'd rarely spoken to us on a personal level. Where Tristan hardly even looked at us, Denise and Ian were friendly, outgoing and welcoming. They were pleased with the difference we were making to the garden which, in turn, made us happy. I say *we*, but really it was Steve who made the difference. I was only the picker-upper.

The weather was beginning to turn and Denise's lawn and small orchard beyond the formal garden were already a splendid, autumnal carpet of muddy-brown, gold and burnt-orange leaves. I spent many afternoons raking, creating enormous piles to throw on the bonfire stack. This wouldn't be lit until sometime in October, though, as it was illegal to have a fire before then. The summers were so dry and neighbours or passersby would report anyone who ignored the rules to the *pompiers* (firemen) who would promptly arrive to douse the fire, giving the offenders an on-the-spot fine.

During September, Denise invited three girlfriends from the UK to come and stay for a few days. The mornings were certainly cooler but the afternoons warmed up beautifully and

the girls spent this time around the pool, topping up their tans.
Topless.

'Heavens, you seem to be doing an awful lot of cutting and
pruning by the pool,' I teased Steve, who jumped at hearing my
voice behind him.

'Well there's, um, there's a lot to be done around here,' he
blustered, suddenly busying himself with the cuttings.

When I was raking by the pool, it wouldn't take long for
Steve to turn up.

'Going OK? Need a hand?' he would ask, trying to look
innocent. I'd never known Steve to be so solicitous, checking
how I was doing. I'd given up saying, 'Stop looking, stop
looking!'

The following day, Steve stayed indoors (not before time),
catching up on admin while I finished raking. Hearing Denise
and the girls laughing and chatting around the pool brought a
lump to my throat and I was overcome with homesickness. I
rested my chin on my hands cupped over the end of the rake
handle and thought of my girlfriends. As well as the usual meet-
ups for coffee and a glass of wine, I especially missed the
impromptu Friday afternoons and evenings we often shared.
Someone would usually suggest we rang the guys to tell them to
come round after work and we'd get curries in for the adults and
pizzas for the kids. They were fun and special times. Steve could
only fill my emotional tank to a certain level but the rest needed
topping up with girlfriend time, chats and 'show and tell' after
clothes shopping.

After a busy day in the garden I'd felt exhausted and taken
myself off to bed early for a quiet read. Denise and Ian had other
friends staying this time. From their living room across the
driveway, I could hear the occasional shriek of laughter and
Barry White's sultry and sexy crooning voice. My book was

instantly forgotten as I lay there and listened. The silly grin on my face would've told a story as I'm a huge fan of Barry White and have an unforgettable memory where he's concerned. On my 40th birthday, my friend Barb arrived to take me to a girls' celebratory lunch. Knowing how much I loved Barry White, she'd pulled up in my driveway in her soft-top Mercedes, the roof down and Barry White belting out at full volume. Barry stayed at full volume all the way down the highway, with Barb and me punching the air and joining in (also at full volume), causing quite a stir with other drivers and when we reached the restaurant.

They must be having a good time over there, I thought, closing my eyes, loving the music. I then heard Denise calling and Steve going to our front door. He stood at the bottom of our stairs, relaying the message up to me.

'Hon, get up. Denise wants us to go over for a drink. The girls are dancing and want you to join them.'

Dancing! My tiredness instantly evaporated. I leapt out of bed, threw some clothes on, swished the mascara wand through my lashes, added a touch of lipstick and ran down the stairs. Steve and I crossed the driveway and whizzed up the front steps. Denise shrieked, 'You're here!' as we stepped into the living room. She thrust a glass of wine in one hand and dragged me into the middle of the floor by the other. And that was the beginning of a very long night.

Dancing was like a distant memory and it was so good to be moving, feeling free and having fun.

Domaine de Ménerque

Domaine de Ménerque cottage

3

French Life

Siobhan introduced us to Anglo Info, a useful website where we subscribed to the Midi Pyrenees South group, getting lots of helpful information and asking questions in the online forums. There I found Doug and Siobhan's French teacher, Andrée, who did one-on-one as well as group classes. I promptly booked myself in as she was in Gaillac and only ten minutes from Denise and Ian's door. With life more settled and winter on our doorstep, I wanted to use the quieter months to concentrate on learning the language. I needed to in order to get involved in our local community and make some French friends and of course Steve would be so delighted to have me learn French, too. I could then stop asking him, 'What did she say? How much was that? Can you read this for me, please? Can you tell them I would like…?'

Most days we drove to our local *boulangerie* (bakery), *La Panetière P'tit Resto*, in Avenue Saint-Exupéry for a *pain aux raisins* (a sweet spiral bread containing raisins and a custardy filling) and our lunchtime *flûte* (a type of baguette that's a bit more expensive, has no additives but has more flavour and a slightly chewier crust). We stopped sometimes for coffee at the Continental on the way. The Conti, as it's affectionately known, is an *auberge* (inn/café) situated on the upper square in the heart of Gaillac. It was one of our favourites and we'd often sit at a table on the terrace, enjoying the coffee and the morning rituals of the locals as they meandered between the butcher and the greengrocer and then on to the bakery. There was always time for a chat with each of the artisans to swap a delicious recipe or news with friends and neighbours they met in the street. A brimming basket would be slung over an arm or a bulging shopping trolley pulled alongside. Life wasn't rushed. This was the daily rhythm and thread of French living in the small towns and villages, completing the embroidery of their lives.

While living at Denise and Ian's, we enjoyed a lot more free time and the luxury of weekends. One Saturday morning we went into Lisle-sur-Tarn to a *vide grenier*. Literally this means 'empty the attic' and is what you and I would call a flea market or car boot sale. The French (and English) bring whatever they want to sell and set it all out on trestle tables in a designated street, field or hall. Colourful bunting is strung up, creating a fête-type atmosphere; live music plays and food and drink stalls with tables and chairs are dotted amongst the trestle tables and in the shade of trees during the warmer months. It's quite an occasion in the French diary and several hundred people always attend, meandering from table to table, hoping to find that very thing they didn't even know they needed. I was one of them.

I adore fabrics and trawling through one tableful of old French linen, I found two monogrammed sheets. One looked to be hemp and the other, thick cotton and only €7 each. What bargains. They were yellowed and marked in places but don't worry, I received plenty of advice on how to get rid of the stains. I would use the sheets as tablecloths with the monogram proudly displayed at one end. I loved them for their history, often wondering who had owned these things and how they lived. I was glad I could repurpose the sheets which would always be a memory of our time in France.

I also couldn't resist two pristine, white, heavily embossed, cotton quilts which were going for a song at €10 each. Steve watched me running the material through my fingers, knowing how much I love textiles and creating a home.

He raised one eyebrow at me. 'Yes, Annemarie? What d'you think you're going to do with those? More importantly, do you really need them?'

'No, I don't *need* them but I do want them. I can lay one across the end of the bed in our guest room, once we get to Merigot, and the other can be a summer throw for our bed.' I just got the rolled eyes and proffered hand to carry my purchases. He didn't really care at all what I bought but couldn't help commenting just to keep me on my toes, or so he thought...

Now that we were staying in France, I was almost nesting, wanting to make our new place a proper home. I was excited about moving into Combe de Merigot and was fervently praying it was all going to work out well after the disaster at Mas de Lavande.

As the weeks passed, the morning temperatures dipped to around 10°C but climbed to 25°C or more, making for beautiful afternoons. Lisle-sur-Tarn was bursting with vineyards, and sun-ripened, juicy grapes were being harvested late and in earnest, either by hand or machine. Most days we could hear the rumbling of the harvesters working their way between the vines. Coming back from town one day, we pulled over to the side of the road to watch the machines trundling up and down, vibrating the grapes off the vines. It was so much faster and far more economical to harvest that way but special vintages were usually picked by hand.

Denise left at 5:00 a.m. one morning to pick grapes with a group of friends at a local vineyard. At sunrise everyone gathered at the cellar door for instructions and the owner handed out coffees and pastries before work commenced. It was hard going, she said, but also great fun with everyone bent, chatting through the vines as they worked. Come lunchtime, with all the grapes in for that day, the barbecue was lit, the wine poured and all the helpers sat down at a long row of trestle tables to a delicious feast as a thank you from the grateful owner, enjoying a glass (or two) of last year's vintage.

Instead of farmers bouncing hay bales along the narrow roads, we now encountered tractors towing huge vats of pungent, sweet grapes, and whiffs of the musty, musky scent filtered through our open windows when we drove behind them. Sunflowers, too, were being cultivated for their seeds and oil and the landscape was changing once again with fields left bereft and sad with decaying, straw-like stalks instead of pert, yellow faces raised to meet the sun.

While we were at Ménerque, Gabriel (the gardener at Mas de Lavande) and his wife, Suzanne, invited us to a *bière dégustation* (beer tasting) at a country microbrewery. About to walk out of the door to meet up with them, I checked with Steve whether we should take a bottle of wine with us. Just in case they didn't sell any.

'No, no. Don't bother. This is France. I'm sure they'll sell wine. Not everyone drinks beer,' was his answer. Well I certainly don't.

But no, they didn't sell wine. Luckily for me, Steve managed to get Gabriel on the cell phone before the family left home and he kindly stopped and picked up a bottle of rosé at the *tabac* (bar/café/lotto shop) for me to share with Suzanne.

With counters set up in shack-like stalls in an enormous, mown paddock, the beer tasting was in full swing when we arrived. The band playing at full volume, combined with lots of noisy chatter from the crowd, created a fun atmosphere. Plates of cheese and charcuterie were being trotted out with the beers to customers standing at make-shift bars enjoying their drinks, perched on hay bales dotted around the place or sitting at barbecue tables set up under cover in the enormous barn. The live band was the highlight and we managed to have a dance or two early evening but after their second stint, where they repeated all the songs from the first session, it was time to go. Time spent with Gabriel, Suzanne and their girls was always fun and by then I'd had several French lessons with Andrée so I practised a little with their eldest daughter who was keen to practise her school-level English, too.

During our time in France, I noticed cheque books were still frequently used. At one of my lessons, I discussed this with Andrée. She thought it was because credit cards were expensive for many people to have and use. I'm guessing she meant the interest rate and the annual fee. From appearances, some people living in the countryside had very modest lives and from our experience of the French banking system, internet banking wasn't often used. If we wanted to make payments online, we would need to ask for the account numbers and codes as they were never offered outright. On many receipts, too, the amount was in French francs as well as euros as so many of the elderly couldn't get to grips with the euro. The French we met were very respectful of their parents and the elderly and helped them as much as they could. I loved this attitude.

4

The Changing Days

Bonjour! Comment ça va? Ça va très bien, merci! (Hello! How are you? Very well, thank you.) See how good I was at French? Hah! That was about as much as I could muster apart from introducing myself and ordering a glass of wine. I was so frustrated. After five lessons I was ready to throw *le livre par la fenêtre* (the book out of the window). Andrée, my *very* patient teacher, told me I was in too much of a hurry and to be kind to myself. Steve (and friends) will tell you I'm always in a hurry and terribly impatient. It was so difficult learning conjugated verbs (whatever they are) and everything being masculine or feminine. For heaven's sake! I knew I'd have to persevere if I was ever to fit in and make any French friends.

That morning, though, and with great joy, I pushed my French homework to one side. There I was in the cottage kitchen, a domestic goddess, cooking up a storm. You could call me Julia Child—minus the apron. The air was redolent with balsamic and red wine vinegars, onions, root ginger and spices as a batch of fig chutney bubbled away on the cooktop. A pot of thick, garlicky pumpkin soup was simmering next to it. With a glut of figs and pumpkins throughout the countryside, it was my absolute duty to cook as I couldn't bear to see the waste. The supermarket was selling figs at €4.95 a kilo. 'Pah! Who would pay that when you must know at least one person with a fig tree in their garden?' she (me) said, with a toss of her head. Figs were falling and rotting on the roadside, they were in such abundance. I can identify a fig tree from 50 paces when it's heavy with ripened fruit as they have such a sweet and pungent fragrance. I'd pilfered these figs from Denise's enormous tree but I did the decent thing and gave her a jar of the chutney.

After a pea-soup-fog start to the morning, I threw open our terrace French doors to embrace the glorious sunshine now pouring in. I stood for a moment on the step, eyes closed, enjoying the warmth on my skin and the delicious aromas wafting from the kitchen, feeling ridiculously happy with my simple life. What more did I need? The radio was belting out some excellent French and English music and I sashayed, hummed and warbled my way around the kitchen, chopping, dicing and slicing, giving both pots a little stir now and again. Cosmo, one of Denise's cats (renamed Pork Chop by me), was a rather large, ginger cat and she lay back, spread-eagled on the sofa snoozing, enjoying the warm sun on her belly. I couldn't help but give her a little tickle and a rub on my way past. Pork Chop was so fat she looked like Garfield the cartoon cat in size, with a tail that was too short for her enormous body. The other cat was Harry, a large tortoiseshell, and nick-named Harry the Hunter as piles of pigeon feathers materialised every day in different locations around the property but never a carcass to be found.

Harry trotted past the kitchen window one morning with a thrashing baby bunny in his mouth. I was horrified. I wanted to rush out to save that poor baby from Harry's jaws but it wouldn't stop him doing it again and again. Steve saw him later that same morning with yet another. The awful thing was that Harry would disappear with these animals through the laundry-door cat flap. I hated to think what remains Denise would have to deal with when she returned as that door was locked and we couldn't get in to remove any dead bodies.

It was mushroom season as well. These varied hugely in price in the markets and supermarkets, depending on their type and whether they'd grown under pine or oak trees. We saw mushrooming fanatics parked up in lanes, decked out in gumboots and waterproofs with baskets swinging, traipsing into the forests in search of these delicate and delicious morsels. Hammered onto lamp posts and trees were rough-cut, timber boards with written warnings, stating which variety was safe to eat. Any mushrooms picked in the wild needed to be verified by the local pharmacist who was trained as part of the job to identify the deadly and the safe mushrooms.

September was the start of *la chasse* (the hunt) and ran every Sunday until the end of February. It was nothing like the English hunts on horseback, horns blaring and a pack of hysterical, baying dogs weaving through the horses' hooves. These hunters were on foot, with one or two dogs close at heel and rifles 'broken' over the crook of their arms. They wandered up and down in the fields right next to us, kitted out in gumboots, camouflage jackets and peaked caps. Every now and then, a resounding crack echoed around the valley as they fired. We could hear the gunshots from dawn until dusk.

I trundled the wheelbarrow full of cuttings to the bonfire stack one Sunday wearing my lime-green, fluorescent top, deliberately making myself highly visible. I certainly didn't want to be mistaken for something tasty. Not very likely was it? Old birds are too tough… It was rather frightening, though.

Speaking of old birds, I'd always relied on my hairdresser, Charlie, in New Zealand to keep me looking respectable and a little trendy. During our months at Mas de Lavande, I had several horrendous haircuts at a local hairdresser's. Now I was not only in need of a decent cut but desperate for a colour, too. Putting my faith in Andrée's recommendation, I booked in with Valérie at Coiffeur Ondul'Hair in Gaillac. What a difference she made. No one would have known grey streaks peppered my hair, and I was now looking *très chic* with a stylish cut. I only wished she could have cut out the multitude of folds in my neck as well. Each time I looked in the mirror, I had visions of Hilda Ogden, one of the scrawny-necked chickens we'd looked after at Mas de Lavande. I wasn't enjoying ageing.

In the meantime, we (read—Steve) carried on with Denise's garden but I did contribute to our set number of hours, to be fair. As well as working in the garden, sometimes I helped Denise in the house, cleaning windows and floors and vacuuming, managing to chit-chat and drink coffee at the same time. Denise and I got on very well and she became a great friend and companion during our time in France. Her French was perfect and she offered to help us out with any French documentation should we need it.

We shared a love of New Zealand sauvignon blanc and Denise created great excitement in our cottage the night she came and joined us with Doug and Siobhan for dinner. In her hand was a chilled bottle of Oyster Bay sauvignon blanc. It was the first New Zealand wine I'd tasted in months and it slipped down very easily—so floral and citrusy and such a treat. Denise and Ian brought this wine and others back when they drove to and from the UK.

While at Ménerque, Steve found a new best friend in the old chap next door. This beaming little Frenchman toddled past Denise and Ian's every morning, his walking stick balancing him on his constitutional. He would call out a cheery *bonjour* and raise his cap to Steve over the hedge. We never did find out his name but he was a delight, always smiling, and took great pleasure in telling Steve he was 97—amazing. He only looked 67 and he put his longevity down to hard work from the age of 14. On his return journey, he would perch himself on the little stone bridge out the front and watch the world go by, waving to all and sundry as they passed on foot or in cars. Sometimes when I was at the clothesline, I would see his wife and him across the field, sitting in the shade at their back door. They reminded me of a Darby and Joan scenario, propped up in their chairs next to each other, or like the little man and lady that popped out either side of those old-fashioned chalet weather houses with the tiny barometer set in the middle. The couple always raised their arms to give me a friendly wave, calling *bonjour*.

When Steve and I were out walking, we'd pass their garden and once while *madame* was weeding, I couldn't help but compliment her on the beautiful yellow crocuses she was growing *and* I said it mostly in French, I might add. She bent over, picked one and handed it to me with a warm smile and a *bonsoir, m'sieur-dame* (a short form of *monsieur et madame*). She was a delight. Other locals further along the road, savouring the warmth of the late-afternoon sun and sitting at their outdoor table enjoying an apéritif, would wave and call out *bonsoir et bon marche* (good evening, have a good walk), *m'sieur-dame*. This was the semi-rural France I loved and where I felt happy and at home.

While at Denise's, we took the opportunity to explore and visit the popular hilltop village of Cordes-sur-Ciel. We'd only ever passed it, never stopping to visit. A steep walk from the main road led up into the heart of the town, but several roads and car parks were created around the hill's side, making access a lot easier.

Many of the boutiques were shut and very few people were around when we went. The tourist season (May/June/July/August) was a double-edged sword with the heat and throngs of people so getting a car parking space or a seat in a restaurant over the summer was difficult. However, the summer tourists were vital to keep the French village economies alive during the quieter months but as it was late September we had no trouble parking. We climbed to the town square and enormous parapet, walking through magnificent, stone-built arches and past old stone troughs now filled with vibrant geraniums and wildflowers. Ivy, turning an autumn shade of orange/red, climbed the outside of stone houses and fig trees sprouted from cracks and crevices in the gutters. Shutters, some peeling and warped after a sun-beating over the summer, were now closed and awaiting repair for the next tourist season. Steve and I stood licking an ice cream, loving the glorious, tree-filled-gorge views across the valley.

Not far from Cordes was Castelnau-de-Montmiral, our next stop. This town, too, was known as one of the most beautiful villages of France and a *bastide* (a fortified town with a central square and a rectangular street layout). It was an impressive stronghold over the centuries. The square, surrounded by corbel vaults (arches built with bricks that support the superstructure of the buildings) was beautiful and the focus of all village life. The town featured in the fifteen-minute film *Now Retired* and showed it off to its best. Nearly every front door had terracotta pots sitting either side and on window ledges, filled with geraniums or other pretty flowers. The views from the paths around the exterior of the village took in the rolling landscape and plots of forests, intersecting roads and dotted farms and homes in the countryside.

That day we could have fired a rifle down Castelnau's main street with absolutely no danger to any member of the public.

'Where on earth *is* everyone?' Steve was turning in circles, looking for people. 'It's so quiet. The online blurb said it was a lively and bustling place.'

'I can see two people in that restaurant but that's it.' I pointed to where a couple sat, having a bite to eat at one of the outdoor tables. I checked my watch. It was 1 p.m. so we assumed everything was closed for lunch and most people were inside, having theirs.

Many English have settled in Castelnau-de-Montmiral, creating businesses and rejuvenating the town, which the local

French people welcomed. During our time at Combe de Merigot, I often came to the village and saw it at its busiest, especially during July and August with its market days and when many evening musical events took place in the lit-up square. Tickets sold out early and people flocked from all over the Tarn to enjoy the different bands and singers.

'Come on, let's get a table and eat. I'm starving.' Steve grabbed me by the elbow and steered me over to the restaurant. He was always starving.

Our exploring often took us to *vide greniers* in the region. At one in particular, we both wanted a good rummage through everything and agreed to meet back at the same spot in an hour.

'Hello, what did you find?' Steve wandered towards me later with his hands full. 'I picked up these French books. I thought it might help if I read the language as well as speak it. They were so cheap—only €1 each.' He looked delighted with his purchases. 'And you?' He stuck his nose into my carrier bag.

'Look at this electric citrus juicer. Only €3! I'm tickled pink. And this cute little sauce jug for €1.' I pulled them out of the bag to show him properly. 'Absolute bargains.' Stuffing them back in, I pointed to the side of the stalls. 'Come on, there's a coffee caravan with tables and chairs out. Let's grab a coffee and people-watch for a while.'

'The awful thing is,' Steve muttered to me out of the side of his mouth, once we'd sat down, 'there's quite a lot of junk here and only a few treasures. I do wonder how much they actually sell.'

'I was thinking that, too.' I grimaced. 'So much effort goes into getting here, setting up and then you have to pack 90% of it away again. It must be worth their while otherwise they wouldn't do it, I guess.'

❀ ❀ ❀

That evening at home, I needed to attack my French homework. My lesson was at 10 a.m. the next day and typical of me, I'd left it until the last minute to get on with it.

Steve slapped his hand down on the dining table, making me jump.

'Right, *madame*, what do you have to do for homework tonight?' I was slumped over my books, doodling on a sheet of paper. He could see I was procrastinating about starting.

'I've got to listen to this dialogue—*in* French. Andrée is going to ask me questions about it—*in* French,' I grumbled. 'I not only have to understand the dialogue, I have to understand *her* and then I have to blimmin' well answer—*in* French! Will you help me?' I asked Steve in a pathetic, wheedling voice.

'Ah no, sorry. You've got to try and do it for yourself. I can't be there all the time to help you with conversations, you know.' Steve's haughty and pompous tone said it all. I swear I heard him give a dismissive sniff, too, as he turned on his heel.

Fat lot of help he was. Just as well he'd turned away and didn't see me silently mimicking him and making rude gestures behind his back.

Would I ever master the French language?

5

Our New Home, Shopping and Snippets

Our full-time job at Combe de Merigot would mean we were making a commitment to stay in France for a couple of years and Steve would need to register to be able to work.

'I've checked the *auto entrepreneur* status, which looks to be the one that covers self-employment here.' Steve was browsing his laptop. 'We'd be responsible for paying our tax.'

'That's fine. We can do that. Mary and Symon will pay us a set amount each month so it won't be difficult to work out the tax. Just the how and when to figure out,' I called from the kitchen. I left him to delve deeper while I finished dinner.

'So if I sign up as an *auto entrepreneur* and pay tax, I then need to register for social security and find a health insurer apparently.' Steve was slowly scrolling through all the information. 'Then we can get our *carte Vitale* and become part of the French health care system. Yes. That'll be us sorted.'

'OK, let's get onto all of this tomorrow.' I pushed a load of papers to one side so I could put our dinner down on the table. 'I should imagine it's going to take a while to come through so the sooner the better. Right now you need to eat this before it gets cold.'

Deciding to stay in France meant rethinking our

arrangements in New Zealand. We would continue to rent out our house there. We knew Callum, our youngest, would travel once he'd finished university in Auckland so we would see him in Europe. But when would we get to see Archie again? He was living in Australia so we'd have to make some sort of arrangement so we could meet up. As for our siblings, well, we just didn't know.

Our start date at Combe de Merigot was the 8th of October and we were due to move in on the 6th.

'Symon has emailed, Steve.' I slid my laptop across the desk to show him. 'He's suggested we have dinner together when he arrives on the 7th. He thinks it'd be a good opportunity for us to start to get to know each other and I do, too.'

'Definitely. Have you decided what to make for his first dinner yet?' Steve teased, knowing how I liked to plan ahead.

I snorted. 'Not yet, smarty pants! I've got plenty of time to sort that, thank you very much. D'you know, though,' I pondered, 'I don't feel at all nervous—not about meeting him or cooking for him for the first time.' It struck me, in that moment, just how true that was and how at ease I felt about our new roles and employers. 'And did you also read the bit where he said Mary's coming down with a girlfriend a week later? They'll be here for four days.'

'Yep, saw that. Great she can get here so soon, too. We'll get a more in-depth idea of how they like things done and start on the right foot.'

We went for another look at Combe de Merigot the week before we moved in so Steve could walk the property with Michel, who'd been looking after the place and the dogs in the interim. After I'd explored the house, I stayed inside the cottage with the excuse of doing some French homework but really I wanted to have a good look around our new home, especially the kitchen, to see what we might need. The cottage was so much bigger than I first thought and the kitchen looked well equipped. The big, solid, stainless-steel double oven with very sturdy gas hobs was new and absolutely pristine. The dishwasher had recently been plumbed in and had never been used so that was perfect, too. I was so excited and couldn't wait to move in. It was all so new, fresh and clean and I was in love with the place before we'd even begun to live there.

Mary emailed during the week.

Annemarie, the cottage sitting room needs some tall reading lamps for the side tables. I'll be getting two of these and we can talk about what you'd like when I see you. When you get there, go ahead and replace the kitchen pots as from memory they're pretty battered. You might also need to buy a new set of decent knives and please help yourselves to the stainless-steel cutlery set in the annexe kitchen. It's much nicer than that in the cottage.

I'm currently working with our interior designer and we're redoing two of the bedrooms in the house. I know there's a surplus of bits and pieces so take a look at what's stored in the atelier and help yourself to anything that will make the cottage more comfortable for you.

We couldn't believe her generosity. *Please, please, please, God,* I silently prayed, *may this be the way our relationship continues.* I couldn't cope if there were dramas and upsets like we had working at Mas de Lavande.

When we moved into Combe de Merigot, the temperature was back up to 26°C with a gentle zephyr blowing after two days of gale-force winds which took the tops off several young oak trees. The long driveway was strewn with branches and piles of leaves, which swirled in clusters in the wind then gathered in dark, damp corners, waiting for me to trundle them up to the bonfire pile.

It was the easiest of house moves: four suitcases, a set of golf clubs and supermarket bags full of groceries. We managed to get the key early morning and moved everything in one go. Denise was kind enough to let us use her big Trooper wagon and Steve filled it with the suitcases and golf clubs and went ahead while I brought all the food and clothes on hangers, following behind in our little Renault Mégane car. It was a quick trip back to Denise's place, ten minutes away, to finish cleaning her cottage and to drop off the wagon. We were done.

It didn't take long to unpack our clothes into drawers, hanging others in the walk-in wardrobe and storing the groceries in the kitchen. I closed the last cupboard door and turned to Steve.

'I just love it here.' I knew I was beaming like a Cheshire cat, opening and peering into drawers, running my hand along the clean lines of the benchtop and eyeing up the delightful blue and white crockery in the white, glass-fronted cabinet. Nothing was chipped or cracked. I shuddered, remembering the filthy kitchen and the crockery I was supposed to use at Mas de Lavande where nearly everything *was* chipped or cracked and there wasn't a complete set of anything. 'I'm sending up silent prayers that it all works out this time, Steve. Mary and Symon do seem such nice and decent people.'

'Well I have a good feeling about this job. And about Mary and Symon. I'm sure it's going to be fine,' Steve assured me, putting his arm around my shoulders. 'Stop looking so gooey-eyed over this new kitchen and let's go over to the house and have a proper look through on our own. I want to take a closer look at that German boiler. I'm going to need to read the manual as it's a monster of a thing.'

We were happily ensconced in our new home, albeit a little sad to be leaving Denise, but I knew we'd be seeing lots of her as time went on. However, nothing could contain my excitement knowing we'd be living somewhere so nice and working in such a beautiful and preserved home. Most of all, working for good people, hopefully.

Michel arrived Saturday to drop off the dogs, Indy and Tilly. Indy was a medium-sized cocker spaniel with the most glorious, glossy red coat and a loving nature. Dear little Tilly, a wiry-coated, grey and white Scottish terrier, had the cutest little black-button eyes. Poor girls. They didn't know us at all and it must have been so unsettling for them, watching Michel drive away. I put their beds in the sitting room and offered them both a little treat. Steve and I deliberately left them to wander around the cottage, smelling our things and sniffing at us. It wouldn't take the dogs long, with us cuddling and petting them, to get used to us and settle down.

Steve disappeared up the drive to collect Symon from the airport while I crossed over to the house, dogs in tow, and made a start in the kitchen and dining room. I'd prepped most of the food earlier in the day and I was all set to go. Tilly and Indy jumped onto the dog blanket on the sofa and promptly went to sleep. I laid the table for the three of us, using Mary's old, initialled linen napkins, French-scrolled dinner plates and side plates and the solid, weighted cutlery. The pretty wine and water glasses from the wire-fronted armoire sat in front and to the side of the plates. I stood back to check how it all looked. Hmm, it needed candles and some greenery or flowers from the garden. I grabbed the candles from the back of the armoire and after a quick recce around the front steps I discovered a few late-summer white roses. Back in the kitchen, I found a little vase under the bench in the scullery, popped the roses in and put it in the centre of the table. Perfect. I was done.

Mary had asked me to get in some supplies so Symon could take care of himself for the second evening. Funnily enough, I still wasn't the slightest bit nervous that his arrival was imminent. Working in a full and properly equipped kitchen added to my calm frame of mind.

Symon had requested a no-fuss dinner as he was aware we'd only moved in the day before. Regardless, I wanted to do something appetising but still casual, starting with mashed broad bean, pea, goat's cheese and mint bruschetta. These were very easy to make and so tasty to have with a drink beforehand. Roasted salmon with a basil pesto topping was the main course. Tiny, French roast potatoes crusted in salt and a little olive oil and a simple orange and fennel salad with Dijon mustard dressing went with it. Individual lemon and orange tarts with mascarpone for dessert would complete the dinner. I had made one extra for Symon to have the following night. I flicked the oven on so I could just slide the salmon in when we sat down with a drink.

I whizzed upstairs to Mary and Symon's bedroom, turned on the bedside lamps and checked their bathroom one last time. I'd hung fresh, fluffy, white towels over the rail earlier in the day and put out new soaps and bath oil, and loofahs and facecloths sat on the ledge at the back of the bath. Everything was ready. Back in the kitchen, I looked at my watch. Steve and Symon would be here any minute.

'Come on, girls. Your daddy will be here soon.' Tilly and Indy leapt off the couch when I opened the stair door, pattered across the flagstone floor and ran down the stairs with me, out onto the drive. Perfect timing. I could see the Range Rover turning in the gates.

Dinner with Symon was comfortable and enjoyable and he smiled and chatted throughout. It was as if we'd known him for ages, so easily did the conversation flow. He was tall and slim with immaculately cut salt and pepper hair and I loved his casual but stylish grooming in a fitted, white, open-neck shirt belted into navy chinos and wearing navy leather loafers. He'd been extremely busy with work and was dog-tired so once the kitchen was clean and tidy and the dishwasher on, it was time for us to leave and give him some space to wind down.

'Before you go, would you like to meet up at 9 a.m. tomorrow for a walk with me and Indy? Tilly won't be up for it but I can show you the best route to take Indy and which tracks to use across our land and those of the neighbouring farms,' he suggested.

'Yes, we'd enjoy that, Symon, thanks. That'll be much easier than walking on the roads, which we've had to do so far.' I turned to Steve as he pushed his chair back. 'We could do with a decent walk. See you at 9, Symon.'

We said goodnight and scrunched across the gravel to our cottage.

'Well, what did you think?' Steve asked as he unlocked and opened the cottage door.

'What a lovely man. I really liked him and he's so easy to get on with. You?' I stepped inside, flicking the kitchen light on.

'Yes, he seems a good bloke. I don't think we'll have any issues. He came across as very approachable.' Steve yawned, climbing the stairs. 'Time for bed.'

On the driveway next morning, Indy was a whirling dervish, such was her excitement to be going out for a walk, with Symon. Off we marched, up hill and down dale, really stretching our legs along the various paths and tracks formed through the farms and hillsides. I spied a huge, gnarly, old fig tree not far from the house, but being October, it was almost bare. I made a mental note to keep an eye on it next season to raid it for breakfast treats, desserts and more batches of fig chutney.

When we'd ventured out to walk at the other properties, it was always on the road and we'd needed to watch for cars constantly. Combe de Merigot was so much better, with several tracks around the farms and adjacent woods, plus some narrow, single-track roads. Tilly would remain behind when I did the big farm walks, though. It would be too far for her little legs and she would be much happier curled up in her bed until we returned.

6

Combe de Merigot

Mary and Symon's French home was beautiful, inside and out. Originally a wine merchant's house from the 17th century, it was built in a pale-pink brick.

Combe de Merigot

Mary engaged the services of a French interior designer,

Catherine-Hélène Frei von Auffenberg (CH to most of us). Under Mary's instruction, they'd converted an expansive country house into a classic and elegant French home. It was large and comprised the main house and the built-on annexe which extended from the main kitchen/sitting room and blended seamlessly. Let me walk you through some of it so that you get a sense of the place.

Combe de Merigot side view

In total, it was an eight-bedroom, eight-ensuite home with an extra powder room. The annexe contained three of those bedrooms, a kitchen and large dining/sitting room.

The main house contained a large kitchen, scullery, dining and living area with doors opening onto terraces on each side. The access to the *pigeonnier* had been walled off to create a warmer sitting room and to provide storage behind it.

A gymnasium, *cave* (wine cellar) and atelier were on one side of the ground floor and an enormous boiler room and separate laundry on the other. Symon's *cave* housed a superb collection of French wines, precisely racked and catalogued, locked behind tall, three-metre-wide, centuries-old iron gates. A beautiful, oval, dark-oak table with six chairs sat outside the gates with crystal decanters, glasses and leather notebooks and pens neatly arranged for tastings.

The winter dining room, drawing room, Symon's office and an expansive foyer covered the middle of the house with five bedrooms housed on the top floor. Beautiful, old stone staircases connected the lower and upper floors on both sides of the house.

Throughout the house, artwork adorned the walls and hallways and exquisite objets d'art and books sat on shelves, chests, cabinets and mantelpieces. Steve was captivated by a beautiful bronze sculpture of a wild boar (known as a *sanglier* in France) and I fell in love with two antique, multi-coloured, parrot candlesticks and many other pieces of art.

Eight antique, black and gold framed herbarium (dried plants or herbs) lined the kitchen walls and I coveted these the entire time I worked there.

Apart from the daily working areas of the kitchen and my well-equipped laundry, the rooms I loved the most were the drawing room and the winter dining room. The large, polished mahogany table, centred candelabra and ten chairs gave a formality to the winter dining room, as did the four curved and carved cabinets with brass clasps and handles placed at various points around the room. Lamps or tall ornamental candlesticks sat on each as well as framed photos or a special piece.

The English drawing room was elegant and comfortable with cosy sofas and armchairs you could sink into in front of the fire, and here again, beautiful pieces of art adorned the walls or sat on low chests of drawers and cabinets along with a multitude of books of every genre.

A highlight of the property was the summer dining room and pool area accessed through a tall, wrought-iron gate set into a high brick wall which enclosed the whole complex.

Combe de Merigot pool

Deep-green, climbing ivy softened the interior brick of the pool area. The dining area, enclosed on three sides, had pretty white roses growing up the fixed trellis on either side of the wide, open side, which looked over the pool. An eight-seater dining table and chairs were centred in front of a large, open fireplace. Two outdoor chairs and a coffee table were pushed back against one of the side walls and a fully equipped kitchenette sat behind an internal wall.

To the right of the pool an outdoor shower, a full bathroom and a lengthy covered area had been built where you could lounge, read or doze out of the glare and heat of the sun.

I adored it all.

Our two-storey accommodation across the flagstone and gravel courtyard was only a couple of years old but blended subtly with the whole property. The roofline was a shallow, pitched style, which extended out at least 12 metres, under which we left our car and where visitors could park beside us. Inside it was modern but with a classic, fresh, English/French feel.

Combe de Merigot front view

Upstairs were two double bedrooms with a spacious, walk-in wardrobe and ensuite in our room. Both bedrooms were classically furnished and Steve hung five pretty plates, each painted with a single, stylised and colourful tulip, in our room and a set of old framed prints to complete the guest room.

Downstairs housed a separate bathroom, good-sized living room with an office alcove to the side and, of course, the kitchen and laundry. An outside door led up to a lawned courtyard that would be our garden.

White-painted, sloped ceilings and massive beams throughout reflected the light and gave a fresh look. The whole place was warm and welcoming and I felt so proud of our new home.

The land surrounding the property was large and made up of avenues and walkways of various tree species as well as several large lawned areas. A raised and bricked border of white rock roses ran lengthways across, in front of and up the double-balustraded staircase at the entrance to the house. It sat at the end of a square lawn, hosting clipped box balls set inside open, wrought-iron, oblong casings placed at each corner, giving a formality to this area. A large field beside the pond was left fallow and wildflowers now grew in abundance.

The rows of vines at the rear of the house ran up the slope to the edge of the forested perimeter and completed the extensive landscaping of the *domaine*. It was a stunning property.

Combe de Merigot in winter

7

Settling In

After Symon's brief stopover, Mary arrived with a friend for a long weekend. It was a pleasure to meet her face to face finally. Her warm and engaging smile reached her eyes and as she came towards me I could sense a gentle nature and a comfortable ease about her. I liked her straightaway. Mary was fair, with a scattering of light freckles over her nose and cheekbones. Her wavy, strawberry-blonde hair, some of which was bunched in a tortoiseshell claw clip on the top of her head, fell halfway down her neck. Dressed in a pastel-pink linen shirt over white, slimline pants and wearing white sneakers, Mary looked casually well-groomed.

Our time together wandering the property and chatting was relaxed and informal. Mary and I had pre-arranged I would cook for three nights and they would look after themselves for one. I'd gleaned from our conversations that the family was fit and very health conscious and once I met Mary and Symon, I could see they looked after themselves.

They weren't complete vegetarians but seldom ate meat, preferring fish and lots of fruit and vegetables. I put together a menu that Mary was happy with for the three nights. They loved the first night's dessert of little chocolate pots with a dusting of ground almonds, served in cute, individual, Wedgewood-blue terracotta pots and the petite lemon custard cakes served in ramekins on night two. Dessert on the third night was taken off the menu!

Mary sent an email when she was back in London, thanking us for taking such great care of her and her friend. They'd enjoyed the food, which made me very happy. Mary was so natural and she and Symon felt (as we did) that we were going to get on just fine. It was early days but what a totally different relationship this was already compared to that with owner Tristan and Sarah, his agent, at Mas de Lavande. Thank goodness.

Michel was still working at Combe de Merigot, helping the interior designer CH paint some of the bedrooms and bathrooms. Each morning they were there, we'd join them in the main kitchen for a coffee. I really enjoyed getting to know CH. She always looked elegant, even in painting overalls, cinched in at the waist with a classy belt and wearing a colourful scarf knotted around her head and either diamond earrings or hooped gold earrings. Her skin and make-up were flawless and I enjoyed her sense of humour. She would regale us some days with stories from her childhood and about her elderly parents who started most days with a glass of champagne. CH was married to Pierre Frei von Auffenberg, an author and a very distinguished gentleman from an old European family.

At coffee one morning, CH was gently removing wads of tissue from a parcel she was unwrapping on the bench. 'Annemarie, would you like to see these?'

'Ooh, what have you got there?' I put my coffee cup down and edged closer to have a look.

'My grandparents owned the most delicate and beautiful glass Christmas decorations. Most of them have broken but I still have five which survived. I arranged for them to be replicated by a company in Belgium and they've done a superb job. Look.' CH held one up to the window. The sunlight caught the glass, making it dance and sparkle as it spun on its ribbon. The round, clear glass was etched with opaque Christmas trees, scenes of children frolicking in the snow and tiny baubles and gifts.

'CH, they're superb.' I reached out to hold the one she was dangling but it felt so delicate and my hand trembled, thinking I might crush the fine glass. I gingerly placed it back on the tissue.

'Mary is getting some for her Christmas tree. They're going to sparkle beautifully in the fire and lamplight.' CH gently wrapped the tissue back around the precious orbs and placed them back in their box.

'They'll look so pretty but I think I'll let you hang those, CH. I certainly don't want to be responsible for any breakages.' I cringed, thinking how awful it would be to break one.

CH travelled all over France buying antiques and newer pieces she made to look like antiques. She and Pierre owned a small *château* with a large garden 40 minutes from Gaillac and often hosted clients and friends at afternoon sales where she would serve wine and canapés.

'After Christmas you and Steve must come up to our home and meet Pierre. I would love you to see my garden, too.'

'Thanks, CH. We'll definitely come. I'd love to see your home now that I've seen what you and Mary have accomplished here.'

With our work routine underway, Steve was keen to get an exercise routine in place. He missed his days out bike riding and after looking at options in a bike shop in Gaillac, he brought a second-hand one home for a test ride. Deeming it fine, he purchased it. Cycling is a popular sport in France with many cyclists using the hill beside us for training and, more often than not, without helmets. Steve was making good use of the gym each morning, too, challenging himself on the rowing machine, the weights and the bench press. I'd been on the treadmill—once. The gym was only across the courtyard but I was lazy and loved to sit having a cup of tea first thing in the morning, catching up on overnight emails and messages rather than huffing and puffing my way around the gym equipment. I easily did 10,000 steps a day working in and around the house so wasn't too bothered.

After grocery shopping one afternoon, I found a flyer under the windscreen wiper when I returned to the car and brought it home for Steve.

'Hon, look at this.' I handed the flyer to him when he came in from the garden. 'The local tennis club is having an open day. I thought you might like to go along for a hit and maybe meet some people? Symon won't mind you borrowing a racquet. There are several in the gym cupboard.'

'I hadn't really thought about playing tennis here but I could go and see what's what. Actually, I wouldn't mind getting back into it,' he pondered, looking through the leaflet.

'Well? How did it go?' I asked Steve when he returned from the tennis club that Wednesday afternoon.

'It was all a bit odd really,' he said, dropping his kit in the laundry. 'It was the first time I've ever played on a clay surface and it was harder and grittier than I expected. I did have a hit with the club coach and asked him about social tournaments and club days. He looked at me a little strangely and said they didn't do any of that. I'm supposed to ring other members and make a time to play.' Steve opened a beer and sat down at the kitchen table.

'But you don't know anyone else. That's the reason you went along—to meet people. That's a bit bizarre. Also, how are you supposed to know who's a good or bad player?'

'Exactly. I told him how it all worked at our club and the tennis evenings we ran—turn up, put your name down and whoever was on duty would draw up a foursome. The coach thought it was a brilliant idea.' Steve snorted.

'Be careful.' I laughed. 'You'll be on the committee before you know it.'

I couldn't play tennis anymore because of an ongoing gluteus maximus problem. It was getting enough of a workout, bending and picking up tonnes of autumn leaves and making beds. Thank heavens for anti-inflammatory tablets.

8

Retail Therapy

Since we'd arrived in France, Steve and I hadn't had a day apart and because of our working life, we were together constantly, so when Denise rang one day with an invitation, I leapt at the chance.

'Hi, Annemarie, it's me,' she trilled. 'I fancy a little retail therapy. I'm heading into Toulouse on Friday and wondered if you wanted to come, too? We could see if Siobhan wants to join us and maybe stop for lunch somewhere. What d'you think?'

'Ooh là là! Yes, let's do it. I'll ring Siobhan and get back to you. Thanks, Denise. How lovely.' I rang off and quickly punched in Siobhan's number.

'Hello, petal. Listen. Denise and I are going into Toulouse on Friday for a little retail therapy and then to have lunch. Can you come with us? It'll be fun.'

'Gosh, I can't remember the last time I went out with the girls and did some shopping. Love to. How exciting. I'll organise Doug to pick up the kids from the bus. Thanks.'

Siobhan and I met at Denise's and after a quick coffee we were back out of the door, piling into Denise's wagon and on our way to Toulouse. Apart from shopping, it was wonderful to be having some 'girl time' as I missed my girlfriends and the time we spent together. Several hours later I was fizzing with that euphoria known to many women as the shopping high. I bought a very smart, navy, puffa jacket for winter walking and a black, military-style wool coat. It was ridiculously thrilling to be buying something new.

As you can imagine, Steve missed me *terribly* that day—not. I'm sure he revelled in being on his own and having peace and quiet. I'm a chatterbox (in case you didn't realise) and Steve isn't, but by the time I returned home, I'd used up my daily 10,000 words—and more. No wonder he was delighted to see me. He assumed he was in for a peaceful evening, the silly man. I can talk the hind legs off a donkey.

My fabulous, floral Joules wellies were another excellent buy as they'd be very useful on sloshy winter days, walking the dogs in the paddocks or the garden.

The autumn days were so beautiful but for me it didn't really matter what the season was. Often while working upstairs in the house, I'd be pulled to the window by an invisible thread and just stand and absorb the glorious view of the rose garden, the trees now almost bare on the curve of the drive, the lush green carpet of lawn and mirror-like pond. The undulating and patterned landscape, dotted with sheep or cows, stretched out to distant black steeples, stone houses, chimneys and a sea of tiled roofs. It was a bucolic, pastoral painting and the window surround its frame. How did I get to be there? How did we get lucky enough to be working and living on that beautiful estate? I couldn't answer those questions but I was grateful.

Late one golden, crisp afternoon, I wanted to return some platters to Siobhan. Instead of heading down to the D999, I took the back road. Turning right at the top of the drive, I followed the road for half an hour through farmland and forest. The low, autumnal sun flashed through the trees, creating a kaleidoscope of red, orange, gold and brown while grey smoke from early-season fires trickled from chimneys, creating meandering pathways through the sky.

As I passed the pheasant farm, I swerved to miss one or two escapees wandering around on the road. These were free-range birds and I felt just like them—free. Our lives had dramatically changed in the past few months and I felt an overwhelming sense of peace and happiness as I drove those back roads. There was minimal stress, time to enjoy a social life and work and to catch up with family and friends back home.

One email contained this lovely little French joke, sent by a friend:

At a dinner party thrown in Canadian Prime Minister Jean Chrétien's honour, an Englishman turned to Madame Chrétien and said, 'Your husband has been such a prominent public figure with such a busy schedule, retirement will seem very quiet in comparison. Madame Chrétien, what are you most looking forward to in these retirement years?'

'A penis,' said Madame Chrétien.

A hush fell over the table and heads turned. Everyone had heard her answer, yet no one knew what to say next.

Jean leant over to his wife and said, 'Aline, in hinglish, dey pronounce dat word, "appiness'.'

9

Animals and Other Stories

'I'm going up to empty the tarpaulin on the bonfire pile,' Steve announced one morning after breakfast. We'd done a major clean-up of the drive and front lawn the day before and the tarpaulin was heavy with garden debris. He lifted his jacket off the laundry hook, slipped it on and disappeared through the back door. The weather was much cooler these mornings and you could feel the chill and sharpness in the air. We were most definitely heading for winter.

At the kitchen bench, finishing my cup of tea, I could see Steve's frosty breath as he bent to pick up the tarpaulin. He jolted, dropping it like a hot potato, and stumbled backwards. A flash of something leapt into the air and disappeared into the woodpile. I opened the window a crack and Steve turned to look at me.

'What on earth was that?' I asked warily, not quite sure what I'd seen.

'A big, fat rat.' Steve was now scanning the woodpile. 'Best keep the back door shut all the time over the next few days. There's some rat poison in the storage shed that I'll put on top of the logs so the dogs don't get it. That should sort it.'

From then on, Indy went mad each time we went out,

clawing at the logs to try and get at the rat so we knew it was most definitely still there. Several days later the poison had disappeared and I was sure the rat was well and truly dead. I did, however, keep our front door firmly closed, just in case. I certainly didn't want to see it run out from behind the couch or have it climb the stairs to our bedroom. Ugh! It didn't bear thinking about.

On our walk across the fields one afternoon, Indy and I came across two large *ragondins* (coypus). They're similar in size to a beaver and are the scourge of the farmers as they destroy the vegetation. One of them ran off but the other stood its ground, up on its back legs, baring its disgusting orange teeth. It was fearless as Indy lunged at it, with me pulling hard on her lead. I was nervous as these things attack other animals with their hideous teeth and long, sharp claws. It would've been horrific if Indy got hurt. I told Denise about coming across these two and one of them standing up on its back legs.

'My God, make sure you keep the dogs well away,' she warned. 'I know of a dog that was attacked by a *ragondin*. The poor thing lost an eye and had its stomach ripped open by the animal's claws.' I recoiled in horror. What hideous creatures. 'As you would expect, the dog nearly died from internal wounds and infection but somehow it survived,' Denise said. 'So just be careful.'

To complete the vermin stories, I got my own fright, clearing leaves in the rose garden. There, slithering through the bark, was a black snake with vibrant yellow markings, quite thick in girth. I had no idea how long it was as I leapt like a gazelle out of the garden but screamed like a banshee, running to find CH in the house.

'CH, there's a snake in the garden! Come and look, quickly!' I grabbed her by the arm and hurried her outside.

'It's OK, it's OK. It's not a viper, just a harmless snake. It won't hurt you.' She calmly patted my arm, peering in between the roses.

That was *mildly* reassuring. That was until several days later in another part of the garden where I *did* come across a viper. They're skinny, brown and short in length. I shuddered. They look innocuous but must be left alone as to get a bite from one is life-threatening. If you do get bitten, the rules say you're supposed to remain calm (well that's hilarious for a start) and walk slowly so you don't pump the poison through your body. Walk slowly? I'd be yelping and leaping about in pain and dead in five minutes. You're supposed to get to a telephone and ring for help. It crossed my mind it would be a good idea to know what that telephone number was.

Taking care of dogs was something very new for us as we'd only ever cared for cats. Tilly and Indy needed quite a lot of attention —Tilly, because of her allergies and eczema and Indy, because she was a never-tiring fetcher of balls and wanted constant love. Steve would be working outdoors somewhere and Indy would arrive at his side, dropping a sloppy, wet tennis ball at his feet. She'd start to back away, waiting for him to throw it. If he didn't do it immediately, she'd pick it up and drop it even closer until Steve stopped whatever he was doing and obliged.

Part of their care was bathing them regularly, especially if they'd been up in the forest and rolling in badger poo or something equally disgusting. Believe me, badger poo has a stench all of its own and it's hard to remove. I'd gag sometimes when it became overwhelming while bathing the dogs. What a performance it was during my first attempt. Steve was out in the garden with Michel when he heard me shrieking in the bathroom.

'What the hell's going on? You OK?' Steve came running inside.

'No! Look at me. I'm absolutely saturated. And look at the bathroom walls! They're covered in filthy dog water. What a mess,' I yelled in exasperation. The problem was a sopping wet Tilly, shaking herself madly before I got a towel over her. As she escaped through the open door with me not far behind, dripping from head to toe, Michel grinned in recognition of what had happened and tried to stifle his laughter. It must have been infectious because Steve started laughing, looking at my soaked T-shirt and jeans and dirty water running off my face. I was the only one not amused. When Michel got ahold of himself, he turned and spoke to Steve who translated for me, still grinning like an idiot.

'Michel says in order to keep yourself and the bathroom clean and dry you must quickly drop the towel over Tilly as soon as you've finished rinsing her.'

This I managed to do after that first disastrous attempt at dog washing but right then and there I needed to spray and wipe down the whole bathroom and dash upstairs and change my clothes.

Indy loved having a shampoo, quietly sitting beside the bath waiting for her turn while I washed Tilly. She was so keen that she would scrabble into my arms as soon as Tilly was done, trying to get in the bath. She would sit in there, with her nose pointed north and her eyes closed, while I massaged in the shampoo. Just like us at the hairdresser's. She was so human in so many ways. In winter I would blow-dry her so she wouldn't get a chill. She loved that and would continually turn in circles, pushing her face into the warm air. She was such a funny girl. I didn't want to sting Tilly's fragile skin using the hairdryer so she just got a gentle pat dry and I'd put an old towel in her bed to absorb any more moisture. They both had such personalities and I came to love them as if they were my own.

Tilly & Indy

10

An Introduction

Our lives got busier the day I met Sarah at the hairdresser's. With her fluent French, Sarah helped explain to Valérie what I would like done with my hair. Sarah and her husband, Richard, own gîtes and have a conference centre and a large home to rent in Castelnau-de-Montmiral. After we'd chatted for a while, we exchanged phone numbers. She was so friendly and very easy to get on with so I sent a text message a few days later, inviting her down to us for coffee. From that morning on, our social life changed.

An email popped up in my inbox.

Hi, Annemarie, thanks so much for coffee on Monday. I was telling you then about the candle afternoon at our place. I wanted to confirm that it's on Sunday week, at 2 p.m. I do hope you can make it. There'll be about eight of us and it would be such a good opportunity for you to meet other women from the area. I've attached a map of how to get to us. Oh, by the way, there's no obligation to buy so please don't feel you have to. Let me know if you can come. Love S

I was so looking forward to it and emailed her back straight away, saying I would most definitely be there.

While at Sarah's party-plan afternoon, I received an invitation for Steve and me to attend a cancer fundraiser evening and for me to join a French/English-speaking group. I'm good at that—the English-speaking bit. Another lady, Jeanne, invited us to the English/French Remembrance service at Castelnau-de-Montmiral and following the service to the annual curry lunch held at her home.

Combe de Merigot was well known and one of the two largest, English-owned properties in the area. Before Mary and Symon bought it, it was available as a holiday rental and the previous owner used to hold large parties which some of the people we met had been to. When the time came for the property to be sold, the owner put on a huge sale of all the house contents. Mary and Symon were bringing their own furniture and furnishings so they didn't need anything. People came from all over the Tarn, not only to buy but also to look through this prestigious property.

Many English homes we were later invited to housed something from that sale. If they didn't, the owners definitely knew of the place. We were often introduced as the new guardians and there would be an audible 'ooh' followed by 'and how are you getting on?'

'Fabulously, thank you,' was always our response. It was true. Steve and I couldn't have been happier. Whatever gorgeous procurement was made at that huge sale would then be proudly revealed to us. It might be a chest of drawers, armoire, curtains, a piece of art; there was nearly always something.

I drove home from the afternoon at Sarah's with a light heart and on a high. I'd enjoyed being with a group of interesting local women and being invited to things. Our social life was underway and I was delighted.

The morning of the Remembrance service dawned cold and

crisp. My coat was tightly buttoned up as we got out of the car at Castelnau-de-Montmiral and I pulled on my gloves and stamped my feet to try and get the circulation going. Steve and I arrived early to have coffee before the service began. Parking beside the Vival store, we headed for the café on the square, passing homes with their front doors sitting directly on the road. It was difficult not to look inside as we walked. Through one window, a book on New Zealand caught Steve's attention. The couple indoors saw Steve peering in so he gave them a friendly wave and started to move on. The window was thrown open, a *bonjour* tossed into the frosty air and a hand thrust out to say welcome.

'Forgive me for staring in. I couldn't help but notice your book on New Zealand,' Steve offered apologetically in French, shaking the hand at the same time. 'We're *from* New Zealand, you see,' he explained.

They were happy to meet us as they'd travelled throughout New Zealand and loved it. We found it hard to believe that there we were in a small town, in the middle of France, and these people had made the long journey to visit our home country.

With *au revoirs* exchanged, we trudged up the steep path to the town square and into the café. A blast of warm air enveloped us as we entered and with each clang of the café bell, heads would turn and wish the new face a friendly *bonjour*. It was no different for us.

'Hello, you must be new here. We're so and so. Lovely to meet you. Where are you from?' Hands were extended and everyone was so welcoming; it was heart-warming. People plonked coats and hats on spare chairs or doubled up on the coat hooks as they peeled off their layers in the heat of the café.

One gentleman looked so smartly dressed, I couldn't help but compliment him.

'Excuse me for being forward but may I say how elegant you look in your pinstripe suit?' I smiled at him. His medals were firmly pinned to his left breast. He looked to be of a similar age to us and turned out to be English.

'You may indeed! Thank you so much. Not forward at all; very nice of you to say so.' He stood even taller, accepting the compliment. 'You're obviously new here. I'm Luke and this is my wife, Catherine,' he said, turning to draw Catherine into the conversation. She was French, with the most delightful accent.

'*Bonjour et bienvenue* (hello and welcome),' Catherine offered with a wide smile.

'I'm Steve and this is Annemarie, my wife, complimenting you. Pleased to meet you.'

'We've ordered our coffee but would you like to come and sit with us once you've asked for yours?' Luke invited. 'There's a free table by the door. A little draughty, I know, but that's all that's left.'

The café door was constantly opening and closing as the place filled rapidly with others who were attending the service and had the same idea.

'We'd love to,' I answered. 'We'll be right with you, thank you, Luke.'

What a charming man. Luke was ex-British Army, now a consultant and also fluent in French. He was one of the English representatives to speak at the service. In our area they would say Luke spoke Parisian French as opposed to the 'Oc' accent (Occitanie, a regional dialect). The Oc pronunciation has a very 'ang' sound at the end of some words. Catherine was an artist and having modest success with online sales.

With coffee over, it was time to layer up again, don coats and hats and with flushed faces from the heat of the café, make our way in procession down through the narrow streets and past half-timbered houses to the memorial at the bottom of the hill.

The service itself was a beautiful commemoration and even though I could only grasp bits of the French, I found it very moving. Luke spoke so eloquently, in both English and French. It was somehow very appropriate to be a grey and chilly day and to have the rather 'mature' local brass band playing for such a solemn occasion. At the conclusion of the service, the mayor invited everyone to gather at the *boulodrome* (boules pitch) for a glass of wine. We toasted all those who'd sacrificed their lives so we could live freely today.

Drinks were dispatched and everyone hurried to the warmth of their cars, driving in convoy to the curry lunch hosted by Jeanne and her husband, David, and attended by about 40 people. It wasn't only for their English friends but also the French mayor and other French people in the community.

The curries were delicious with so many people contributing different flavours and choices. We mixed and mingled and also continued our conversation with Luke and Catherine. Lunch was a bit of a dine-and-dash, though, as Steve needed to get Symon to the airport. We exchanged contact details with Luke, thanked our hosts effusively and hurried out of the door. Luke emailed the very next day.

Annemarie and Steve, we very much enjoyed your company yesterday and would like you to come for coffee. We're returning to the UK tomorrow but once we know the dates we'll be back in France, I'll get in touch and we can set it up. We do hope you would like to come. Speak soon. Luke & Catherine

How lovely! We'd so enjoyed meeting them. From the curry lunch came an invitation from another couple to go to theirs for dinner and for Steve to go and play golf. Finally he got to play his first game on French soil, at a course called Palmola. He enjoyed a great day out with the guys, starting with a village breakfast on the way.

'Hello, how was it all?' I asked as he came through the door late afternoon.

'Brilliant. Everyone was good fun but my golf was rubbish. I was hopeless and struggled on the greens.' He was annoyed with himself.

'You haven't played for about nine months. What did you expect? I'm sure you'll be a lot better next time and at least you had a great day with the guys.' Golf is such a fickle game.

All in all, we were delighted to be meeting people and socialising again.

11

New Ventures

Symon returned to us from New York on his way to visit the London office and his home for a few days. He loved to be hands-on when he could and he and Steve spent the afternoon clearing bracken and fallen trees, cutting some into firewood and hauling the rest to the hidden bonfire pile. Mid-afternoon I set up a tea tray, adding muffins straight from the oven, and carried it up to the back paddock.

'Wonderful, Annemarie, thank you. Just what we needed.' Symon smiled gratefully, hauling off his gardening gloves.

We found a spot to sit and I poured, handing round the tea and muffins. Indy was having a lovely time, following Symon and Steve around, snuffling and rootling under bushes with Tilly sauntering along behind her. Now they slumped beside Symon, Tilly immediately dropping off to sleep and Indy resting her head on her paws, watching Symon.

'While we're together this is a good time to talk to you about a bit of a plan Mary and I have hatched. I want to run it past you.' He put his cup back on the tray and leant back on his elbows.

'Oh? This is interesting.' I sat up, keen to listen. Steve was looking quizzical, wondering what Symon was about to suggest.

'You piqued Mary's and my interest when you told us about your involvement in the artists' workshops and art club week at your previous place.' Symon waved his hand in the direction of Brens. 'We're thinking of holding yoga retreats, interiors and antiques weekends, cuisine and cultural weeks. That sort of thing. Here at Merigot. Of course I need to look at the financials of it all but Mary and I wanted to see how you would feel about us opening up the house. You would be fully involved, of course, and it would be a partnership/business arrangement with a profit share.'

I was stunned and it took me a moment to digest what he was saying. 'Heavens. I would love that. The house and grounds are perfect for it. How wonderful! What d'you think?' I turned to Steve.

He took a minute. 'Well, it would certainly add another dimension to our job and really, it was exactly what we wanted from our first role here in France,' Steve explained to Symon. 'There's a lot to think about, that's for sure.'

'There's an *awful* lot to think about,' Symon agreed. 'Why don't you email me and Mary, setting out how it all worked plus anything else you think might be relevant? I'll talk to Mary later on the phone but she and I will thrash it out when I'm back in London. The four of us can then talk about it more thoroughly when we return in a few weeks. That will give me time to draw up a marketing plan and work out the financial cost of it all, including public liability costs and to set some pricing.'

How exciting! Working with Mary and Symon, we knew everything would be well thought out, properly planned and executed to a professional standard.

Back in our cottage, I was getting dinner underway as we talked, while Steve sat at the table making notes.

'We'd have to put away all their personal bits and pieces. And the office would have to be locked,' I said over my shoulder, stirring the curry.

'And the wine cellar,' Steve mused. 'We can't have any of that disappearing. It's too valuable.'

'The atelier is so perfect, though, isn't it? For yoga classes, I mean. Ooh, what about painting classes in there, too? We could contact Shelley ourselves and ask her. She'd be easy to find in Richmond. Remember her? The art tutor who ran the workshops at Mas de Lavande? She'd be brilliant. And she's very professional,' I rattled on to Steve, snipping the ends off the green beans, ready to throw them into the curry.

'Yes, she was excellent. I'll add her to this list for our chat with Mary and Symon.' Steve busily recorded everything.

'Also, these ventures don't have to be limited to just summertime, you know, Steve. Spring and autumn are beautiful months and some guests might even prefer winter events. There's plenty of hiking, horse riding and other activities to be enjoyed in cold, sunny weather,' I pondered, turning to look at him. 'Hey, we could ask Domaine Duffau down the hill if they would be interested in hosting wine tastings, too. Mary and Symon know the owners. I'm sure they would be delighted to.' This was getting very exciting.

'Yes, we could do,' Steve agreed, slouched in his chair, thinking and chewing on the end of his pen.

'We've got four huge fireplaces here; imagine toasty afternoons and evenings around the fire. Plus there's a vast DVD and book collection, should the weather close in. This is just what we wanted, Steve. My mind's whirling with ideas.' I was almost hugging myself in anticipation of all the things we could offer.

'Yes, well, just calm down, you. There's a lot to talk and think about before anything can even be confirmed. After dinner, why don't you start that email to Symon? Then you and I can both go over it before you send it. That'll get the ball rolling.'

Symon drew up a plan for marketing and promoting these weeks. Emails flew back and forth across the Channel. He was onto someone in New York to lead the yoga sessions and suggested CH could lead the interiors and antiques, cuisine and culture events. Her skill set was impressive—interior design, cook, historian, antiques and a fount of all knowledge. CH was so quintessentially French but fluent in English. She could also host antique events at her little château and garden and we could take guests to places like Conques to explore the area and its history and little boutique restaurants CH knew of off the tourist trail. Included in these tours would be the markets in Toulouse and Albi. The guests could be introduced to the best chocolatier, *fromager* (cheese merchant), charcutier and other artisans.

On the list would be guided tours of the 13th- and 14th-century parts of Toulouse, including a private home with one of the most exquisite furniture and art collections in France. After being in the business for 30 years, CH had a significant portfolio of contacts and clients.

Sitting at the computer, composing my email, I sat back, my arm slung over the back of my chair.

'Ooh, just imagine, Steve—beautiful summer evenings, dinner set for 12 at the long trestle tables in the tree-lined "avenue", you know, at the side of the house. In full leaf those treetops meet and form a wonderful canopy. It's so sheltered there. I'd cover the table with Mary's antique tablecloths, put out the hurricane lamps, silver cutlery, the crystal wine and water glasses and thread ivy through it all. We could even string fairy lights between the tree branches. It would look amazing.'

That was me gone, into my fantasy world, picturing exactly how I would 'tablescape' it, how it would all look and planning menus to boot.

'Then what about this? Early evenings you could drive guests on the back of the 4x4 up to the ridge above the vines. They could sit on hay bales, enjoy the stunning views of the vineyards and countryside. Hey, we could even serve champagne and canapés from the deck of the wagon,' I went on. 'What d'you think?'

'I think you're a romantic fool, that's what I think.' Steve grinned. 'You're just going to have to be patient.'

'I know, I know,' I agreed reluctantly, feeling a little deflated. I couldn't help it. Combe de Merigot was the most perfect place and I couldn't wait to get started and show it off.

Symon was pitching this at the high-end market. Pricing for the all-inclusive weeks or weekends would be rather expensive but I knew it would be worth every penny as the house was unique and so beautiful. It oozed elegance and comfort and was also very French and in the countryside. What more could people want? There were exciting times ahead.

Perfect weather greeted Mary and Symon on their arrival with their adult son and daughter, and they were able to get out walking with the dogs, relax in front of the fire and unwind from their hectic working lives. Tilly and Indy always moved into the house when the family came. Both of them would go silly on the drive as soon as any of them stepped out of the car. It was lovely to witness.

Before Mary left either New York or London, she would send me a list of what groceries they would like and I'd do a big shop at Leclerc in Gaillac to have everything to hand. My role for that long family weekend was to cook dinner for two nights only, after which they would look after themselves.

During their first afternoon, Steve and I had a good few hours with Mary and Symon, talking through the proposed weeks and weekends at Merigot and how it would all work. On the last day of their stay, they popped over to the cottage to see us.

'Right, I've been through everything—financials, marketing plan, injury waivers and lastly public liability insurance. We're sorry to disappoint you but after thinking and talking long and hard about it all, we've decided we're not going ahead,' Symon explained.

I think I must've physically slumped in my chair.

'I can see you're disappointed, Annemarie, but the public liability insurance cost is horrendous for a start,' Symon said. 'We'd have to charge a king's ransom to make it a viable proposition.'

'Then each time the house was booked, you two would have to pack away all our personal possessions and some of the more valuable paintings and objects,' Mary added. 'Once the groups left, you'd have to unpack it all again for when we come over. It's an awful lot of work. I know we were going to get commercial cleaners and others to do the hard graft then employ people to do the airport pickups as well as you, Steve,' Mary pointed out, 'but we both feel it's just too much. When it comes down to it, it's our home for our family and friends to enjoy. There would be a lot of wear and tear, too, beyond our control.'

'Our intention at the start of this plan was to make the place start to pay for itself,' Symon explained. 'Now, having gone through the process, it's not about the money. The place wouldn't feel the same to us after strangers had been here. We'll just carry on the way it's already working. Sorry, both.'

I was quiet for a moment, thinking. 'Please don't even begin to apologise, truly. We totally get it and you're quite right. From the start it's been a family and friends place for you, rather than a commercial environment. I was just excited about what we could offer guests and where we could take them exploring. CH came up with some brilliant options as well. But really, we understand. It's much better this way—and thinking about it, our lives will be a lot easier, too.' I smiled at them both. 'It's absolutely fine.'

Steve drove the family back to the airport late afternoon and each time they left now, I was sorry to see them go. They were good company; even though they were our bosses, they always had time for conversation with us.

That night we received an email.

I know you're both disappointed we're no longer proceeding with the yoga retreats and other events but they're just not viable. Steve and Annemarie, we wanted you to know, though, how delighted we are with everything at Combe de Merigot. Mary & Symon.

It was a shame but made perfect sense. Yes, we were delighted, too. We were truly enjoying our job and country life in general. Looking after the house, leaving each room ready and beautiful for the next visit and cooking for the family was a pleasure, not a chore.

12

A French Home of Our Own

Each morning, weather permitting, I'd be up the drive and walking a road circuit with both dogs and sometimes Steve. We'd start at the top of the drive, walk a short distance uphill, watching for traffic, then turn into a quiet, single-track road. On we'd go on the lesser country roads until we turned down to the main road which led back up to our driveway.

En route our walk took us past the Canto Perlic vineyard, small land holdings, several B&Bs, the duck farm and everyday cottages. I fell in love with one of these cottages and always stopped to admire it. Its position was just perfect, sitting proudly on a small plot. A stand of parasol pines was on the right-hand side with a small, open paddock on the left. A white picket fence with a gate in the centre surrounded the property. The whole place was like a child's drawing. With its A-frame roofline, the stone cottage presented a central, red-painted front door with a rose-arbour surround and large, recessed and shuttered windows either side. A short but meandering garden path led from the gate to the pretty door.

On a clear, sunny day, the backdrop was the sparkling, snow-covered Pyrenees far, far away in the distance. It could easily have been a framed painting. From the side paddock, we could see the rear of the cottage and the sizeable covered deck with two sets of French doors opening out onto it. The deck was big enough for a six-seater table and chairs as well as two outdoor chairs. I often imagined myself sitting there, glass in hand, drinking in those fabulous views. I knew I'd never get tired of them.

I noted on the letterbox the name of the people who owned the place. 'I'm going to live there one day,' I said to Steve. It hasn't happened—yet. As Steve often refers to me as Detective Inspector Rawson, I decided to do some investigating and discovered it was only used as a holiday cottage by the owners. On one of our walks, I slipped a note in the letterbox which gave our contact number and email address, letting the owners know how much I loved the cottage and expressing our (my) interest in purchasing it, should they ever wish to sell.

A month or so later, an email popped up from them. Sadly they wouldn't be selling soon as they, too, loved the cottage and used it often. They lived in Folkstone, England, and often came across to enjoy a break in the Gaillac region. They did promise to keep our details and would get in touch should they ever wish to sell.

You need to know that during this time the ever-sensible voice of Steve jabbered in my ear, 'We're NOT buying a property in France. We live in New Zealand. It's just not practical or fiscally sensible.'

So? Was my silent, belligerent answer. I loved that cottage (even though I hadn't stepped a foot inside) and wanted to buy it. My heart was ruling my head. Yes, alright, alright. I knew what he said was correct. Don't go on. As I write this story, I haven't heard from the owners again. I might just send them another email. Just to keep up the contact, you realise...

Speaking of buying a property in France sight unseen, I met a lovely woman, Rebecca (not our cook/chef friend Rebecca), in a café in Toulouse on one of my trips into town. She was from London and somehow we started talking and got on famously, swapping emails and phone numbers. She and her husband bought an old stone house, sight unseen, in the department of Gers. They'd surprised themselves as they were practical people (and fiscally sensible—unlike me, according to my husband) but fell madly in love with it online. I could understand that.

Sadly Rebecca's mother became desperately ill in Guildford and they'd been unable to get down to France to see the place since they bought it. Three months later they finally arrived at their French house. I got a message from Rebecca a few days afterwards. When I opened the email, I must have made some sort of strangled noise.

'What's happened?' Steve asked.

'This email is from Rebecca. Not our Rebecca. The woman I told you about that I met in the café in Toulouse. Remember?' My eyes were still scanning the email.

'Vaguely,' Steve answered, not remembering at all.

'Well listen to this. I can't quite believe it.'

Hi, Annemarie,
We finally arrived at the house two days ago. We love her! She's so grand and such a village focal point. However, we're still a bit shocked to be honest as we found the place totally stripped out. The previous owner took all the lights, lightshades, bulbs and fittings, leaving wires hanging from the ceiling and wall sockets. There's no heating as she drained the oil tank dry, which also means no hot water. She's taken the whole kitchen, and I mean whole—no cabinets, no oven, no hob, nothing. So we're cooking in an old pot and boiling water on the barbecue. She's even taken the toilet roll holders. What's that about? There's not one set of curtains left hanging or a door handle in place. I couldn't believe it.

There was more about the *brocantes* (flea markets) and *vide greniers* they were visiting to try and replace things and get the house habitable again on a strict budget. It was shocking.

'That's terrible. I know a lot of French and Italian house sales include taking the kitchen but this is ridiculous. Have they spoken to the real estate agent?' Steve came over and stood behind me to read more.

'Yes, look further down here.' I scrolled through the email. 'They're waiting to hear back from her.'

I sent off a quick reply to Rebecca expressing our disgust at their awful nightmare.

A few days passed before another email came in from her.

Imagine, Annemarie, if you bought a house and arrived to take possession. You find everything's been taken, including the kitchen sink! No curtains, curtain rails; everything gone. There was nothing we could do and as much as we were horrified by what she'd done, we still loved the house.

So we started a deep clean of the place. Both of us needed to make it feel ours, at least on some level. I'm not going to say exactly where, but we found a secret compartment inside a cupboard. My husband pressed this lever and a door sprang open! Hidden inside was a box full of jewellery, all tangled up. Both of us were stunned. You read about this, don't you?

I've attached a photo. Tell me what you think? I'm certainly in no hurry to contact the old owner to let her know what we've found. Apparently she left the property a year ago and only returned the week before we settled. That was when she stripped the place out.

I gasped, looking at all that gorgeous jewellery, sparkling and glittering—dark-blue sapphires, cut diamonds and deep-green emeralds, all set in silver. On closer inspection, you could tell it was costume only. Rebecca and I went back and forth talking about what to do while she checked for any markings on all the pieces. Sadly, there were none. I so wished the jewellery was genuine as it would almost be compensation and karma for everything that was stripped out by someone so selfish and cruel. How could you do that to someone?

Another email came in two days later.

Guess what? We awoke to no power at all today. We spent our morning talking to EDF. As we hadn't received an electric bill since we officially owned the place, we called the agent and asked if the previous owner let EDF know that the house had changed hands. The agent came back and said it hadn't been done but that the old owner was doing it yesterday. But, Annemarie, guess what she did? She terminated the entire contract and didn't tell EDF that there were new people at the address. If we're lucky the power may be back on Monday. It's Saturday morning, for God's sake! Our new freezer, which we've already half filled, is now defrosting. How could she be so thoughtless? First she strips out the house of fundamental things and now this. I'm so upset.

I was fuming on their behalf. Steve's first reaction was, 'They need a lawyer. This is too much. Firstly, nobody should hand a house over in that condition. Secondly, the agent has been negligent in not inspecting the property on settlement day.'

Even though it was a horrible start for Rebecca and her husband, I was so envious. Why couldn't *I* have a French home of my own? I would love fitting it out with all my *brocante* finds, creating a place where we could welcome friends and family, having long Sunday lunches in the garden. I sighed deeply.

You know why. That damn annoying voice was still in my ear…and I'm sure you realise it wasn't my own.

Rebecca and I exchanged further emails where she told me they'd formally written to the agent expressing their outrage at all that had happened. I hoped they could get everything sorted and be compensated in some way.

Come mid-November and after talking with CH, Steve and I began making travel plans. CH told us the Christmas markets in Munich were the best in Europe and if we were going anywhere to see a Christmas market, then that was the one. Steve had never seen Munich. I was there in my early 20s and remembered the Glockenspiel, but that was all. The B&B we booked was just a ten-minute walk from the markets in Marienplatz. For a brief time, we entertained the idea of going by train but it would take 13 hours each way which was too long. There was too much to be done back at the house to prepare for Christmas and the family coming on the 21st of December.

Steve and I were looking forward to spending Christmas with friends in Saint-Laurent-d'Aigouze, near Nîmes. Our host, our friend Rebecca, who was such a tremendous help to me at Mas de Lavande, was such a gourmand, we knew we would return to Gaillac with expanded waistlines from all the rich and delicious food. Oh, the joys of Christmas.

13

Munich in Winter

The rugged and snow-covered peaks of Mont Blanc rose dramatically through the dense cloud during our flight to Munich. The landscape below was a Christmas card, with snow blanketing roofs, fields and chimney pots. Our pilot wasn't sure if we would land on time because of the weather and it definitely got a little bumpy as we touched down. All this snow was a huge novelty for us.

My bottom was nice and toasty from the heated seats on our train journey from the airport into town, a sensation I'd never experienced before. It was -1°C outside and supposed to be -5°C that night. We rattled past cute chalets with steeply pitched roofs, dotted here and there in the extensive farmland.

As soon as we'd stowed our bags at the B&B, we were out exploring the streets. Dressed warmly in coats, hats and gloves, we watched the snow as it drifted down, melting quickly away on landing. The exclusive boutiques looked very elegant with exquisitely dressed windows while others held festive items of baubles, wrapped gifts, Christmas trees and beautifully boxed and wrapped chocolates and hampers overflowing with wine, crackers, nuts, Christmas puddings and other goodies.

The Christmas market huts (replicas of little Swiss chalets) were bursting with all manner of decorations for sale—intricately carved wooden ones, fragile glass ones as well as the everyday festive baubles. Then there were the food stalls—chocolate-covered fruit skewers, stollen, pretzels and *Baumstriezel*. The latter is a Hungarian pastry, cooked over a fire then coated in cinnamon. Of course there were endless sausages, too. It was so hard to choose.

Some of the little shops in our street were so inviting. Sitting in the café closest to our B&B was like being in a friend's sitting room. It was so warm, with a fire roaring in the grate, and elegantly fitted out with deep armchairs, lamps, bookcases and pretty chandeliers. The delicious, sweet fragrance of warm pastries, fresh cakes on the counter and steaming hot chocolate was mouthwatering.

The department stores, such as Lodenfrey, were a feast for the eyes with all the luxury goods on display. You could smell the expensive leather in the shoe and coat departments, and I couldn't help but run my hand discreetly over the perfectly folded pile of the softest cashmere jerseys and down the silky scarves hanging like ribbons from a rack. I made sure I didn't disturb a thing as I didn't want to risk a glare from the rather severe and immaculately groomed sales people.

It was so refreshing to discover individual stores with quality goods and not the usual city chains. Elegantly dressed women in full-length or three-quarter-length fur coats, with matching hats, passed us by; their leather boots and handbags matched, their makeup flawless. I was probably staring in envy. The men were equally well-groomed, kitted out in full-length wool coats, leather gloves, handsome scarves and some with a sort of trilby hat. Other women wore full-length woollen coats and traditional hats with feathers in. Then there were the thousands of tourists who looked the same as us—very ordinary and certainly quite drab in comparison.

One of the specialty stores I particularly loved was the Dallmayr delicatessen. It was heavenly and a replica of Harrods' food hall but on a smaller scale. The food looked as fabulous as the décor. Enormous, ceramic, cylindrical coffee urns with a ceramic lid and crest for a handle were hand-painted, depicting colourful flora and fauna scenes on the outside. The *fromagerie* chiller groaned with shelf upon shelf of cheeses from around the world. I wanted to open the door just to stand in its frame so I could smell it all.

Customers took a ticket and formed an orderly queue at the charcuterie counter where finely cured meats lay in ribbons or layers on pretty platters. Fat sausages of every flavour were stacked in rows; oily, green and black olives glistened in deep white bowls; potted meats in ceramic pots sat with the lids partially open to entice you to buy; thick layers of solidified butter covered pâtés; pickles and plump gherkins rolled around in brine, and whole, glistening sides of smoked salmon were all displayed beautifully, making everyone salivate just looking at it all. Then there was the bread counter... It was time to leave!

Nightfall came early and Marienplatz was a magical place to be, illuminated by the decorative street lamps, fairy lights strung from chalet to chalet as well as the brightly lit bulbs creating silhouettes of reindeer, Santas and sleighs erected on building façades. Store windows were strategically lit, too, to highlight all the beautiful goods on sale. Christmas music softly tinkled from camouflaged speakers and the excitable cheer and chatter of shoppers was contagious.

On the square we spotted Rischart, a particularly enticing café. It was time to indulge in a hot chocolate. We entered on the street level and passed beautiful gateaux, chocolates and gingerbread, all flavours and shapes, displayed on the counter and just begging to be eaten. The seating area on the second floor was bustling but we managed to squeeze ourselves around a little table overlooking Marienplatz through the floor-to-ceiling glass. This level's counter, too, was groaning with intricately made gingerbread houses, hanging gingerbread ornaments, and chocolates of every variety. The miniature cakes and gateaux looked mouthwatering. Everyone came through the doors hauling off layers of clothing, with cheeks pink from the outdoor chill, and left with cheeks still pink from the heat inside.

On our way through to Marienplatz the next morning, we stopped to look at the *Viktualienmarkt*, a daily food market and square in the centre of Munich. The aroma from the many varieties of sausages grilling was so enticing. We fought the temptation, holding ourselves back until lunchtime when we would taste one or two.

Steve and I claimed a spot in Marienplatz, sipping a hot, fortifying cup of glühwein and looked up to watch the historical Glockenspiel come to life. The square was rammed with hundreds of other people, all doing the same thing.

Every day in winter at 11 a.m., it chimes and comes to life, re-enacting two stories from the 16th century. It consists of 43 bells and 32 life-sized figures. The top half of the Glockenspiel tells the story of the marriage of the local Duke Wilhelm V to Renata of Lorraine. In honour of the happy couple, there's a joust with life-sized knights on horseback, representing Bavaria and Lothringen. The Bavarian knight wins—every time, of course.

The bottom half and second story, the *Schäfflertanz* (the coopers' dance), then swings into action. According to myth, 1517 was a year of plague in Munich. The coopers danced through the streets to 'bring fresh vitality to fearful dispositions'. They remained loyal to the duke and their dance came to symbolize perseverance and loyalty through difficult times.

The whole show lasts about 12 to 15 minutes, depending on which tune it plays that day. At the end of the show, a small golden rooster at the top of the Glockenspiel quietly crows three times, marking the end of the spectacle.

The glühwein was a sweet, almost syrupy drink and a little decadent at 11 a.m. Time to move on. I dragged a semi-compliant Steve into one of the elegant department stores. He patiently waited while I tried on hats and one of those wide, knitted bands that keep your ears warm.

'What d'you think of this?' I turned this way and that in front of him.

'It looks good. At least it will cover your lobotomy scar,' he quipped, snorting at his joke. I just turned my back on him and sullenly hung the band back on the hook. He got the message.

The tantalising smell of sausages cooking got too much for us so we backtracked to the *Viktualienmarkt* to choose our lunch. The food was a bit too stodgy for me—sausage and potato, pork and potato, dumplings and beef. I tried some of Steve's sauerkraut and wondered how anyone could describe that soggy, vinegary mess as a vegetable. My fat sausage in bread, though, with a little mustard down the side, was delicious.

After lunch we wandered in and out of tiny boutiques, one being a teeny-tiny chocolate shop with the entire space little more than a door-width wide. In a very cramped area, the shop attendant managed to create wonderful chocolate delicacies and the sweet and earthy chocolate aroma was irresistible. The full cabinets so narrowed the shop, we needed to turn sideways to get to the rear of it where these pure, creamy delights of every flavour imaginable were for sale. Shelves were crammed with chocolate shapes and pretty-coloured packages of every sort. It was superb.

Every shop window was fully dressed for Christmas and with the freezing cold and snow, you couldn't help but be in the Christmas spirit. We discovered a store called MyMuesli, selling only muesli. It was hard to choose from fat-free, full-carb, low-fat, cyclists' or build-yourself-up muesli and so the menu went on. What attracted me was the packaging and wall-to-wall, floor-to-ceiling display which was so colourful.

Many menswear shop windows were displaying lederhosen, some with very brief leather shorts. For the last 30 years, Steve had been very fond of wearing what we called stubbies— a sort of rugby short—when he was at home. He would have worn these out to dinner if he thought he could get away with it. In New Zealand I found it embarrassing if our friends dropped in and caught him in them. To make it worse, he insisted on tucking his T-shirt into them. Got the picture? It doesn't take much imagination to realise what a sight he was. He got a lot of ribbing. At one significant birthday dinner for Steve, six of our friends (men and women) arrived at our door, dressed in black stubbies with their black T-shirts tucked into them. We nearly collapsed with laughter, watching them file in. They brought going-out clothes with them but Steve told them there was no need to change; they looked perfectly attired as they were. He would!

While in France these shorts were his favourite attire when working around the property and I'm sure our French workmen were smirking behind their hands. All French tradespeople proudly wear a uniform of thick drill trousers, often with a reflector strip down the side.

Sorry, I've gone off-piste. There we were, looking at lederhosen…

'Hey, how about I replace my stubbies with a nice pair of these?' Steve pointed at the lederhosen on display, keeping his eyes firmly on the window and not on my horrified face.

'Don't be ridiculous, Steve! You'd have our French workmen wondering about you.'

'I'm winding you up. I know how much you hate me wandering around in my stubbies,' he joked. Ain't that the truth.

No visit to Munich is complete until you've been to the Hofbräuhaus in the heart of the old town in Marienplatz. It's the most famous beer hall in the world and was established in 1589 by the Duke of Bavaria and can hold up to 5,000 people. Sadly it was mostly destroyed during WWII and needed to be rebuilt but we could feel its history and it still retained timeless elements such as the beautiful paintings of fruits and vegetables stretched across the ceiling and lit by iron chandeliers the size of street lanterns.

On entering, we were struck by the noise level, the sheer number of people and the blast of heat after the cold outdoors. The hubbub of it all created an exciting atmosphere. The Hofbräuhaus covered three floors and, at a guess, there would have been 1,500 people on our level alone. Table after table heaved with visitors from all over the world, most drinking huge steins of beer. The oompah band played at full volume with trumpets, horns and flutes tooting, hooting and whistling and cymbals clashing. Every time the band were about to take a break, they played a particular song which translated as 'one, two, down the hatch!' Everyone stood, clinked their enormous steins (or small wineglass, in my case) and yelled, '*Prost!*' (Cheers!) and then poured gallons of that amber liquid down their throat. It was so much fun and we wholeheartedly joined in.

Space was limited so we squashed in wherever we could. No one seemed to mind squishing up that little bit more on the rustic bench seating, some of which had been there for over 100 years. Karl and Hans, two enormous lumberjacks, were at our table. They were such big men, both German, chatty and good fun. They'd come to Munich for the Deep Purple concert and were in fine form. On our other side sat a sullen young couple. She was from Belgium, he from Lichtenstein. Their long-distance romance apparently wasn't easy. She said he got irritated with her as she read his emails and texts but she didn't trust him. He was angry, told me he loved her but she was driving him away with her jealousy. Heavens! We only went in to experience the beer hall and its atmosphere, not to be relationship counsellors.

Karl and Hans departed, with kisses for me and a crippling handshake for Steve. Taking their place was another Karl with his wife, Sophia, and brother, Günter. They, too, were entertaining and interesting people. They lived on the border of Switzerland and Germany. This Karl was also a brute of a man. What did they feed these people? He was bald, 33 years old, married for 5 years to Sophie and couldn't believe we'd been married for 26. His parents were divorced and it seemed most of his friends' parents were too. We all chatted about our work and daily lives. Somehow I always manage to hear peoples' life stories in a very short space of time. Steve would have you believe it's because I ask too many personal questions. That's so not true…

All three were desperate for a cigarette.

'Annemarie, would you mind looking after our bags?' Karl asked. 'We're going outside to smoke.'

'Course not; no problem. Go, go.' I shooed them towards the door. Karl had been shopping and searching all over Germany for a particular leather jacket but hadn't been able to get one in his size. Really? I wasn't surprised. XXXL must be hard to come by. Finally he'd found his jacket in the elegant Lodenfrey store.

Karl was nearly at the door before he turned and walked back to me. He leant in and whispered, 'Please, Annemarie, do keep a very close eye on it. My jacket was rather expensive. It cost €1,200.'

I nearly choked on my mouthful of wine. What an awful lot of money. My hand gripped that bag very tightly, and my eyes constantly scanned the room for any bag snatchers, until they returned.

We came out of the Hofbräuhaus fizzing. It was like the United Nations inside and the camaraderie was exhilarating. I was so relieved, though, that no one called 'fire'. You wouldn't survive the stampede to get out.

It was bitterly cold at -2°C when Steve and I joined the queue for the Hop-On/Hop-Off bus the next morning, a great way to see the city and get our bearings. One of the highlights was the Nymphenburg Palace sitting at the end of a very long, leafless (in winter), tree-lined avenue. Under an azure-blue sky and a blindingly bright sun, the avenue was a stark and sharply in-focus vista. A semi-frozen canal ran down the centre and the sun, shimmering off the snow pushed hard up against the banks to keep the traffic flowing, was dazzling, reflecting off the bus windows. The palace loomed larger and larger the closer we got, looking like something out of a fairy tale.

The entrance doors were locked when we arrived so we walked to look at the rear, expansive, parterre garden. Under a heavy blanket of icy snow, the perfectly symmetrical garden plants glittered like jewels in the sun. The lines of fir tree branches hung low, heavily weighted with snow. I expected to hear them snap at any moment. All the statuary and some plants were tightly wrapped in a protective cloth to avoid damage from the ice and freezing temperatures. Nymphenburg's garden and interiors mirror Versailles but aren't quite as opulent.

What looked like a greenhouse was a very elegant café-restaurant set inside an enormous conservatory. The exterior walls of floor-to-ceiling glass enclosed in a black, steel framework gave guests a wonderful view over the garden. I pushed the door open and immediately a warm cloak wrapped itself around us. With hot chocolate ordered from the impeccably dressed waiter, we sat back to enjoy the sumptuous surroundings. Striking black and white stone floor tiles were laid in a diagonal pattern, and tall, potted palms strategically placed created a screen effect and added an old-world ambience and warmth. Heavy and ornate crystal chandeliers hanging from the ceiling tinkled and sparkled each time the door opened.

Once off the bus, Steve and I spent the rest of the day on foot, taking in the sights. We walked the elegant street known as Maximilianstraße, watching the well-to-do emerging from the boutiques with store bags weighed heavily with luxurious purchases slung over crooked arms. The Christmas decorations in every boutique were stunning, the best being the Jimmy Choo store where gold and silver balls of varying sizes framed the doorway and an enormous, pure-white bow was centred above the entrance. Maximilianstraße is home to every high-end brand and draws the rich and famous from around the world.

Sunday was our museum day and on the last Sunday in the

month all Munich museums were free. We started with the Deutsche Museum, which held an incredible variety of machinery, including miniatures of the French, American and Russian spaceships, moon buggies and spacesuits. It was a fascinating place but we would've needed days to do it justice. Next on our list was the Munich Modern Museum. Life-sized objects sat in backlit recesses on one of the enormous walls that ran the width and height of the building, housing a car, a motorbike, a three-seater sofa, dining table and many other objects. It was so cleverly done and extremely eye-catching.

Everything combined to make our stay so memorable and Christmassy, especially the snow. So many people were out and about in the evenings, enjoying the hustle and bustle of the beautiful markets, the delicious food, the music and the hot glühwein. Our few days away were brilliant but it was time to return to Combe de Merigot.

Why Did the Chicken Cross the Yard?

What a dreadful day. I was out of the door at 7:50 a.m. in -3°C temperatures to collect Denise and drop her at the airport. Leaving Steve, Tilly and Indy snug and warm inside our cottage, I crawled the car to the top of the drive, hunched over the steering wheel, attempting to peer through the thick fog. The heating was on full blast to try and keep the frost off the windscreen. I flicked the hazard lights on and slowly inched my way down the road, lightly touching the brake every other minute. My insides were constantly changing places in fear. I was terrified of hitting black ice.

Before I left home, my phone had rung. It was Denise.

'Annemarie, I'm so sorry to drag you out in this freezing weather. Please be careful coming over to me. The roads will be lethal,' she warned. 'You just park here and we'll take my Jeep to the airport. We'll be safer in that.' Denise had picked us up more than once from the airport and I was returning the favour.

'I'm leaving early, Denise, as I'll be inching along the roads. I'll ring you if there's an issue. See you soon.' *I hope.* My last two words were a silent prayer.

I arrived at Denise's in one piece, having travelled at a snail's pace all the way. I could see her Jeep was already running in the driveway, with the heater on, melting the ice on the windscreen.

As we drove through her village of Lisle-sur-Tarn, we came across two accidents. One was partly blocking the road and took an interminable time to get past. I felt so sorry for the little old man, looking so shaken standing next to his badly banged-up car but a policeman was looking after him. It looked as though he'd slid into the rear of the vehicle in front.

The traffic was just crazy on the motorway and it took us so much longer than usual to get to the airport. Even though everyone was going slowly, there was still a nose-to-tail accident in front of us. We arrived just in time for Denise to board her flight. I foolishly managed to get myself lost on the return journey in the fog and traffic but eventually got my bearings and onto the right motorway home. My heart thumped after a mild panic of 'how do I get home from here?' and my head pounded with an awful headache from being so tense while driving in the fog and on icy roads.

By mid-afternoon the fog clouds thankfully parted like a set of theatre curtains and the sun burst through, raising the temperature to 3°C. I needed a vigorous walk to clear my head and Indy needed a good run. I pulled on my very glamorous floral gumboots, my very glamorous padded jacket and my not-so-glamorous beanie and grabbed Indy's lead off the hook. I could see Steve through the hedge, bent over the ride-on mower down at the garage.

'Steve!' I yelled, cupping my hands around my mouth. 'I'm taking Indy for a walk. I'll be about an hour. See you soon.'

He raised his head and gave me the thumbs-up. I strode out across the paddock, hands tucked into my thick pockets, crunching along on the still-frosty grass with Indy leaping and yelping in excitement at being out in the fresh air. I felt the same way and took a few deep breaths. It was crisp and cold but the sun was shining in a pale, watery blue sky and it was good to be out.

For most of her walk, Indy was allowed off the lead. Symon had shown me where I needed to put her back on it as we approached certain farms. Indy had previously killed one of the neighbouring farmer's chickens and poor Symon had gone with cap in one hand and a bottle of whisky in the other to apologise.

Indy was generally pretty good with me and returned when I called but that fateful day, she belted off around a bend in the hillside. She could smell something I couldn't. I yelled and yelled for her to heel but I couldn't see her and she wouldn't return. As I got to the bend, I could see a cloud of white feathers flying through the air. *Oh my God.* It was déjà vu. Four chickens were running for their lives down the hill as fast as their spindly legs would carry them. Three managed to scoot under the fence into their yard but the fourth wasn't so quick. I felt sick to my stomach when I saw Indy launch herself, managing to grab it by the throat. Somehow, though, that poor baby got away and ran and ran. Indy gave chase and whacked it down with her paw, clamping her jaws once again around its neck.

I flew down the hill behind her, screaming like a banshee.

'Leave, Indy, leave!'

She took not one bit of notice, so caught up was she in the game. Suddenly Indy got up, walked away from the chicken and came towards me, her tail between her legs. She knew she was in big trouble by the tone of my voice.

I quickly grabbed her, put her back on the lead and hurried her home. I was half running, half walking in my angst to return, find Steve, hop in the car and rush down to the neighbours' house. I stopped in my tracks. To say what exactly? Steve would have to do the talking; they were French neighbours.

I was upset and wringing my hands with worry by the time we got in the car and went up the drive. From the passenger seat, I could see the chicken lying in the paddock.

'Oh no, Steve, look, oh how awful, oh that poor chicken, oh no, what are we going to say?'

'Calm down. These things happen in the countryside. They'll understand.'

Well, I named that chicken Lazarus. As we drove further down the hill, I saw it get up and slowly wobble towards the fence line.

'Steve! It's on its feet. Quick.'

We pulled into the neighbours' driveway. I kept an eye on Lazarus while Steve knocked on the door. Unfortunately no one was home. I could see Lazarus had stopped and was standing under a tree. I didn't want to approach and check if it was OK. That would've added more stress to the poor thing. We left it where it was.

Back in our kitchen, I paced up and down, feeling very anxious about the chicken. I can't bear for any animal to be hurt. Half an hour later, we went back down the hill again. Still no one was home. I swear I saw a white thing in the half-light, lying against the fence, further along the paddock. Lazarus was no longer risen from the dead. He most likely died of shock.

We returned that evening to speak to our neighbours and deliver the bad news. By this time, it was pitch black so we couldn't see Lazarus but could see lights on so knew the neighbours were home at last. Steve knocked on the door.

'*Bonsoir, M'sieur-dame,*' Steve said, as the door opened. He continued in French. 'We're the guardians at Combe de Merigot, Steve and Annemarie Rawson. While Annemarie was walking Indy the dog this afternoon, Indy attacked one of your chickens. We're very sorry. We're not sure if it's alive or dead but we'll replace it.'

Standing there, jiggling from one foot to the other, feeling very nervous watching the proceedings and partially hidden behind Steve, I was expecting a frosty response. When Steve finished speaking, both *monsieur et madame* gave the typical French shrug.

'That's OK,' *monsieur* responded in perfect English. 'These things happen in the countryside.'

God, that's exactly what know-it-all Steve said.

'We're Olivier and Clothilde.' He indicated his wife behind him. 'Very pleased to meet you. Would you like to come in for a drink?' Olivier asked, opening the door wide.

Seeing the table set, it was obvious to me they were about to sit down to dinner so simultaneously, I said, 'No, thank you,' and Steve said, 'Yes, please, that would be very nice.' Honestly he's got no sense of timing, that man.

We ended up staying for a drink and an enjoyable half hour with the charming Olivier and Clothilde and their young children. They were both school teachers and had lived in the area all their lives.

I guess that's one way to meet the neighbours. Not one I wanted to repeat.

15

Our Christmas Build-Up

Since we'd returned from Munich, my days at Combe de Merigot were filled with Christmas food shopping, housework and preparing dishes for the freezer. The house would be full for Christmas when the family and some extended family came to stay. For New Year, their son had invited six of his friends to visit and share in the celebrations.

Mary emailed lists of food she would like me to buy and also had a request.

Annemarie, I know you're busy but would you possibly have time to do some quiches or tarts for the freezer, please? As you know, we've got extra family coming to stay at Christmas and then all the young ones coming for New Year. It would so good to have something pre-prepared for lunches. Mary.

I responded.

Yes, of course. I'm very happy to do that. I'll do a couple of vegetarian quiches and how about a salmon one and a ham and cheese? I can do a Mexican bean chilli too. It's delicious and has chocolate, cumin and cinnamon in it. Something different and handy if you have any complete vegetarians staying. What d'you think?

Ping! Mary was delighted.

So I filled the freezer. In went vegetarian bakes, Mexican bean chilli, leek and goat's cheese tarts, a salmon one, a ham and cheese tart, a citrus flan and a chocolate terrine. I was on a roll. I decided to make a couple of batches of caramelised onions and some lemon curd which could be on standby should Mary need extras. I loved seeing the jars stacked in the fridge and the freezer shelves filling up with good food. I wanted Mary's Christmas break to be as stress-free as possible so she could enjoy the festivities, too. She would only have to take something out of the freezer first thing then bung it in the oven at lunchtime to fill hungry mouths. I enjoyed doing all that cooking as there was time and I didn't need to do it all at once.

Another task was to glaze a ham for Christmas lunch. I'd been given a delicious recipe, known as Pavarotti's glaze—orange juice, brown sugar, honey and mustard. I would smother and baste the ham with this, leave it to marinade overnight then baste it several times more during the cooking process. It has the most amazing flavour.

At the Victor Hugo Market in Toulouse, Maison Garcia is a well-respected Spanish *charcutier* and CH told Mary it was the best place to buy the Christmas ham. My shopping list was quite long so Steve and I took the Range Rover into town to buy this precious meat and pick up other goods. What a mistake.

Victor Hugo market is a foodie's dream to shop at, with a quality restaurant on the top floor, but is in an old part of the city. Read—narrow streets. Navigating them and the even narrower car park in the Range Rover was very stressful—and I wasn't even driving. It was difficult for Steve to get enough swing in the wheel to enter the car park. Adding to the difficulty were cars parked on either side of the road at the entry point and I worried Steve was going to scrape Symon's beautiful car. Each of the spaces was tiny and made for small European cars, not enormous Range Rovers used in the English countryside to cart horse tack around.

There were only about five spaces for large vehicles.

'Quick, Steve, there.' I pointed to the only big space left.

He put his foot on the accelerator, swung the steering wheel around and belted into the parking space.

Oops. A lady, stopped a little in front of the same parking spot, was about to reverse into it. Out she got, presenting herself at Steve's window. *Oh God,* I thought, shrinking lower into my seat, *here we go.*

'What do you think you're doing? This is my park. I was here first,' she flounced, in French.

'Excuse me, *madame*,' said Steve in a conciliatory tone. 'We have a large vehicle and can only park it in one of these five spaces. Yours is much smaller and could fit in any one of these other parks.' He waved towards several empty spaces.

'So why do you have such a large vehicle?' she inquired petulantly. 'Please move and allow me to park there.' I was surprised she didn't stamp her foot.

By this time a queue of starting-to-seethe drivers had formed behind us as the market was hectic at Christmastime. Car doors opened and people got out, craning their necks to see what was going on. The man in the car directly behind us approached. You can imagine what I was like by then— horribly embarrassed and bright red, making myself as small as possible in the passenger seat. I hate this sort of thing. He rattled off something in French, shouting and wildly gesticulating at the woman while I yelled at Steve, 'Move, just move!'

Suddenly it all resolved itself. *Madame* sniffed into the air, tossed her head, turned on her heel and returned to her car. Handbrakes were released; we stayed parked in the larger space and the snake of cars behind us moved forward in an orderly fashion, each to locate a parking place of his own. Heaven knows what the man said to *madame* but it worked. Phew! Glad that was sorted. *Now, where do we buy this wretched ham?*

A few days later, we were off to Albi. On the Christmas list was an enormous rack of beef, an eye fillet and free-range chickens. There would be no upset or arguing with French ladies in this car park. The Albi butcher's shop was beside a huge, modern car park with spaces plenty large enough to accommodate Range Rovers. Symon had rung and ordered all the meat so we just needed to collect it. No stress, no bother. By then I'd lost count of the number of people coming and going and needing to be fed at Combe de Merigot over Christmas and New Year. All I knew was that it would be busy and the house was going to be full.

16

Firewood, Pine Scents and Christmas Decorating

In the middle of all this cooking and shopping, I gave the bedrooms and bathrooms the once-over: polishing taps; cleaning windows, light fittings and skirting boards; making hospital tucks on the sheet corners; straightening bed covers and plumping pillows so all would be sparkling clean and rooms inviting when everyone arrived. Steve's list of chores was as long as mine. He was busy cementing in and rigging up two long clotheslines for the household, clearing gutters, trimming hedges, removing the last of the fallen leaves and getting the firewood sorted.

Doug gave Steve the contact details of a new supplier for dry firewood.

'You'll have to listen hard when you ring, Steve,' Doug advised. 'These two "boys" are local and difficult to understand. They're twin brothers, early 80s and as fit as buck rabbits. Wait until you see them in action. Oh, and you'll need to measure all the fireplaces first. These guys are professionals and they cut the timber to fit, then deliver and stack it for you. All part of the service.'

We were impressed. Eighty years-plus old and still going strong.

Steve decided to visit them to place the order. That was far easier than struggling to understand the local 'ang' dialect on the phone. After winding his way down a dirt track, past truck-high stacks of drying logs, he came to a halt outside a rather ramshackle farmhouse. He knocked on the door and found the 'boys' butchering a cow on the kitchen table. Steve couldn't believe his eyes, seeing these men in bloody aprons with huge knives in their hands, not killing it but cutting it up for the freezer. It was the last thing he expected to find at the lumberjacks' home. He spent a bit of time explaining and miming his requirements and was then offered a little red wine (it was 10:30 a.m.) which he politely declined then left them to it.

Five days later a large truck inched through the gates and rumbled down the drive, drawing to a stop under the hangar and in front of our cottage. The firewood had arrived. It was perfectly cut to measure and I've never seen firewood so beautifully arranged. These two 'boys', one with a mushy, roll-your-own cigarette stuck to his lower lip, kept up a smooth, steady rhythm from trailer to stack, nattering to each other the whole time, for about two hours. That woodpile was a work of art by the time they finished.

Beaming cries of '*merci, madame, merci!*' greeted me when I set down the tray of coffee and chocolate cake onto the now-empty truck trailer. With their hands clasped around the little cups of steaming coffee, they exchanged a few words with Steve between mouthfuls of cake. I smiled benignly, listening but not understanding a word of what they said. I could definitely hear the 'ang' of their accent—what sounded like 'bong matang' for 'good morning' instead of the crisp, French '*bon matin*'. Steve told me they thought he was a Parisian, so impressed were they with his French accent.

From then on, each time I opened the back door the pine-forest scent filled the air. It was heady and so Christmassy and I inhaled deeply every time I passed that wood stack.

The Christmas tree arrived next, along with a sharp blast of freezing cold air as it was manhandled through the double front doors. Steve settled it into the stand in the grand foyer and CH spent all the next day dressing not just the tree but the entire house. How beautiful and festive it all looked. The tree was resplendent with ornaments, ribbon, lights and the new Belgian glass decorations nestled amongst the branches. In every room the fireplace mantles were covered in great swags of greenery, conical pinecones and scented candles. An enormous fir wreath, studded with red berries and ribbon, hung on the front door and Steve had filled the wood baskets and fireplaces with the fragrant logs. It all looked and smelt divine.

All we needed was the family and music, the fires and candles lit, delicious smells wafting from the kitchen and the fragrance of Symon's cigars filling the air. It wouldn't be long. I was excited and couldn't wait for them all to arrive. Every room was ready, freezer and fridge filled and shelves stacked. One last supermarket shop for perishables and I would be done. Steve and I were looking forward to our first Christmas there in the cold and, hopefully, snow.

Our festive season began mid-December with a carol service in the 16th-century church at Castelnau-de-Montmiral. After being warned the church was under renovation and it would be freezing cold, we pulled on thick coats, hats, scarves and gloves to keep as warm as possible. Everyone inside the church was similarly dressed and our breath steamed and hung in the frosty air. Doug, Siobhan and the children came with us. It was a great night of carols, interspersed with readings from the children. After the service everyone was full of bonhomie, smiling and shaking hands with fellow churchgoers as we gathered in the chilly village square for mulled wine, warm mince pies and a chat, while stamping our feet to keep warm.

Jack Frost was starting to bite so Steve and I excused ourselves, shook hands again with all and sundry calling '*Joyeux*

Noël (Merry Christmas) and hurried back to our car, making the short journey home to the warmth of our cottage.

17

Distressing News

A few nights after the carol service, we were walking out of the door, off to enjoy a pre-Christmas dinner at Sarah and Richard's, when Steve's New Zealand mobile rang. My heart leapt into my throat. It was only ever going to be some sort of emergency or problem back home. *Please don't let it be about Archie or Callum*, I silently prayed. I couldn't bear to think something had happened to our sons.

Steve's eyes relayed his fear. 'It's Simon.' He hit the green button. Simon was our brother-in-law, married to Steve's sister, Margot. Steve turned it to speakerphone so I could hear.

'Simon, hi,' Steve said. I could hear the worry in his voice.

'Um, hi Steve.' There was a quaver in Simon's voice. 'Listen, Margot has broken her arm.' My immediate reaction was *is that all?* Relief flooded me. His next words, though, filled us with dread.

'The problem is, when they X-rayed her they found shadows within the bones. The doctors are 95% sure she has bone cancer.' His voice cracked delivering that last sentence. With my arm around Steve's waist, I pulled him in even closer. We were rocked to the core. Margot was all the family Steve had as four immediate family members had passed away in the past six years, the last being his father only 14 months before. It was the most dreadful news.

'Margot's going to have a full body scan tomorrow and...and then she sees the specialist...the day after. I'll call... I'll call as soon as we know any more.' Simon was struggling to finish his sentences, with the tears caught in his throat. I was crying, listening to him. Steve murmured something back. I don't remember what. We said goodbye and hung up.

I could see Steve was struggling with the news, thinking the worst and of the family he'd already lost.

'Steve, d'you want to stay in? Maybe we should talk about what we need to do?' I suggested, trying to comfort him.

He stood there looking at his feet, not saying anything for a minute.

'No, no, there's nothing we can do right now.' He gave himself an almost imperceptible shake and stood up straight. 'Let's wait until we hear back, once Margot's seen the specialist. We can make decisions then. C'mon, Sarah and Richard will be waiting.' He locked the door and turned to the car. Neither of us uttered one word all the way to Sarah's, both of us deep in thought.

Their home was a half hour away, down a long, narrow lane and about a kilometre off the main road. As we came to a stop outside the garages, the house looked so inviting with the warmth of lights filtering through the curtained windows and the outside light leading us to the wreathed front door.

Eight of us sat down to eat in their large dining room. Sarah is a superb cook and produced the most wonderful food. Our first course was parsnip and pear soup with Stilton cheese and the softest little white bread rolls. Roast beef with horseradish sauce and all the vegetable trimmings was the main, followed by an apple and blueberry crumble with cream for dessert. We were all so full but it was a fabulous night, with good conversation and a great distraction from our awful news.

At 1 a.m. we trundled back up the lane and there, caught in

the headlights in the black of night, was a fawn, crossing right in front of us. She wasn't at all frightened and stopped as we came to a halt. She looked up at us momentarily, her ears pricked, her black button eyes glittering in the light and her warm breath frosting in the cold air. She then slipped quietly into the forest. It was a beautiful and surreal moment.

Back home in the cottage, I put the kettle on, thinking Steve might want to talk.

'Cup of tea?' I offered, putting my arms around him.

'No, no thanks. It's late. Let's just go to bed,' he said quietly. I could see his mind was elsewhere as he started up the stairs.

I was sitting with my elbows on the kitchen table the next morning, a cup of tea in my hands, staring out of the window but not really seeing anything, thinking about Margot and everyone at home, when my phone rang. It was Siobhan.

'Hello, you. How was dinner last night?' She sounded bright and cheery.

'It was just lovely, thanks. Sarah and Richard had gone to a lot of trouble and the food was superb. Everyone there was good fun, too, so it was a great evening and a good distraction.'

'What? Why was it a distraction, Annemarie?' I explained about the call from Simon and the awful news about Margot. 'Oh heavens, I'm so sorry,' she said, much subdued. 'How's Steve?'

'I've left him to have a sleep in. We didn't get in until late. He's OK, I think. You know what most men are like. They don't say much about this sort of thing.'

'No, no, you're right. They don't.' Both of us were quiet for a moment.

'Sorry, Siobhan, you didn't know about this so you must've rung about something. What can I do for you?' I tried to be breezy and to lighten the mood.

'Oh yes, right, well as you know, Mum's over for Christmas and there's that much food here it's falling out of the fridge and the cupboards. We thought it would be fun if you could come for dinner tonight. Doug Senior's coming over, too. You're heading away on the 23rd so I thought we'd better see you before you leave. I know it's last minute…and well, you know, with the news of Margot, you might not feel like it…' She trailed off.

'How sweet of you. Look, give me half an hour and I'll call you back when I've spoken with Steve. He's probably awake now with the phone going and me talking. Won't be long, OK?'

'Sure, sure, no problem. Speak soon.'

I went back upstairs to our bedroom. Steve was lying there with his hands behind his head, staring at the ceiling.

'Who was that?' he asked as I plonked myself down on the bed. I filled him in on the conversation.

'We don't have to go if you don't feel like it. They'll understand.'

'No, I'd like to. It'll be nice with the family so say yes. I'm getting up now. I want to finish digging in the poles for the clothesline this morning.' Steve threw the bedcovers back. I could tell he wanted to keep himself busy and didn't want to talk any more about Margot.

It was another great evening with Doug, Siobhan and the family, exchanging gifts and enjoying delicious food and drinks. Their daughter made us a beautiful, timber Yule log which I placed on our window ledge when we got home. Anyone who came to the cottage would see it on their way inside. The only other Christmas decorations in our home were six red baubles hanging on tapered red ribbons in the window. We didn't need anything else; the main house was gloriously festooned with Christmas decorations and both of us were in and out of it so often, we just enjoyed those.

18

It's Beginning to Look a Lot Like Christmas ♫

Mary, Symon and their children arrived, spilling out of the car and into the mêlée of barking dogs going crazy, leaping about, weaving in and out of everyone's legs. The chilly air was filled with excited chatter and frosty breath from us all as we hugged and kissed hello, hauling bags and suitcases out of the boot. Their lives had been so hectic leading up to Christmas and relaxation was high on the agenda. They're an active family so their downtime always included workouts in the gym, runs, yoga, long walks with the dogs then reading and catching up on some TV and DVDs.

This Christmas stay followed the usual pattern for their visits. I cooked for them on the first night and while I finished off their dinner, Symon poured a drink for all of us with Steve joining in. We caught up on their news and updated them with what had been happening at Merigot and the surrounds. It was all so informal.

'Each time Mary and Symon are here and we spend time with them, I have to pinch myself,' I said to Steve as we crossed the courtyard back to our cottage. 'We need to remember that they're our employers and be very aware of that fine line.'

'I know. It's very tricky not to step over it.' He laughed. The four of us got on so well and they were very casual with us. Mary told us they were the lucky ones but we knew the real truth.

The next afternoon Symon stopped at our door with Indy in tow on his way to take her for a walk. 'Hello, sorry to bother you. I hope you're home this evening because I've been sent over to tell you drinks are at 6 p.m. in the drawing room and we must insist that you join us.' Simon delivered his message with mock sternness, grinning idiotically. 'You'll be off early in the morning so we won't see you until your return next week.'

It was always difficult to say no without sounding rude, besides which, he mixed a mean and intoxicating martini, which Steve adored. Can you see me frowning? I couldn't drink it. It was like liquid fire in my oesophagus and one sip made me cough and splutter.

'We'd love to, thank you very much,' Steve said graciously. 'See you at 6.'

'Marvellous! That's settled. See you then.' Symon scrunched his way down the drive with Indy at his heels.

Mary and Symon had been so good to us since we started working for them and Steve and I wanted to show our appreciation. I'd bought Christmas presents for everyone and having a drink would be an excellent opportunity to give them.

The drawing room was beautiful in daylight with the sun filtering through but there was something very magical about it in the evening: the thick and heavy curtains drawn against the cold night, the fire roaring, the soft lamplight illuminating the stunning paintings and antiques as well as having the dogs curled up on the couches. It was so nice to be part of it. As Mary and Symon opened their presents, they seemed delighted with what I'd chosen. Our gift to Mary was a stunning Flora & Fauna Cavallini & Co calendar. The quality of the paper and print was outstanding and each page could be framed. I knew Mary loved gardens and birds just from the sheer number of books in the house on these two topics. In Munich, at the exclusive Dallmayr, we'd bought a Cuban cigar for Symon.

'How did you know this was my favourite brand?' He smiled at us. 'I'm going to keep this and smoke it on Christmas night.'

We didn't know if it actually was his favourite brand but Symon had such beautiful manners, he would never say otherwise. His exquisite marquetry cigar box on the sideboard in the winter dining room stocked an ample supply.

The small gifts for their son and daughter were appreciated, too.

Mary came out of the dining room with presents for us— bottles of champagne, Harrods' mince pies and chocolates and a beautiful, large, winter-scented candle from The White Company in London.

'Mary, this is too much. You really spoil us. I'm embarrassed.' My cheeks were flushed pink. Their generosity and thoughtfulness were quite overwhelming.

'Don't be. We wanted to get these things for you. Merry Christmas, Annemarie and Steve.' She raised her glass.

We all joined in, saluting each other and chorusing, 'Merry Christmas!'

The following morning I was able to relax and prepare to leave. I'd ticked all my jobs off my list and everything was ready and waiting for the arrival of Christmas Day. We'd filled the log baskets and neatly stacked the rest of the firewood. All gardens and lawns were looking good and Steve had done a thorough tidy-up of the workshop so it looked immaculate should Symon decide to use any of the tools. More family was due to arrive that afternoon. I'd even managed to make a last-minute pavlova for Symon's mother.

Everything Mary might need was there. The special Iberian ham, studded with cloves and gleaming with the Pavarotti glaze, was tightly wrapped in cling film in the fridge. All it needed was another dousing and basting of the glaze as it cooked and Symon's knife skills to slice and present it.

Our little Renault Mégane was packed with our bags, wine and presents ready for our Christmas in Saint-Laurent-d'Aigouze. I was locking the cottage door when Mary came across the drive, dogs in tow, wrapping her long cardigan tightly around herself to ward off the cold.

'I know you're about to head off for Christmas but do you two have plans for New Year's Eve?' she asked, bending down to pat Indy.

'No, we were just going to play it by ear and see if anything was on locally. Why d'you ask, Mary?'

'Well, you know we've got a group of young ones coming over to celebrate here at the house,' Mary said. 'Symon and I are going to be the only older ones sitting down to dinner with them all. D'you think you could come and spend the evening with us? We'd love to have you there. You'd be doing us a favour.'

'Oh right, well I think we could manage to help you out there,' I replied drily. 'What d'you think, Steve?' I raised an eyebrow at him. 'Dinner in the winter dining room, New Year's Eve with Symon and Mary and the young set?'

'Fantastic! We'd love that, thank you.' Steve slammed the boot on the last of our stowed bags.

'But only if we share the cooking, Mary,' I insisted. 'Otherwise, we can't come.'

'Fabulous. And yes, I'll take you up on that offer. Let's sort it out when you're back on the 28th. I know Symon has plans to cook this huge haunch of meat for everyone. Heaven knows how it'll fit in the oven. Have a safe trip and a wonderful Christmas Day.'

It was 8 a.m. on the 23rd December as we pulled out of the gates, rolled down the hill and got on our way to Saint-Laurent-d'Aigouze where we'd be staying with our chef friend Rebecca. She'd come to Mas de Lavande at the very beginning of our time there, when I was in such a state about cooking at the house and for a crowd. She's an amazing cook and helped me devise menus for large groups.

Ginny (Rebecca's cousin) and her husband, Dave, were

coming from London for Christmas, too, as well as other friends. Ginny and I have a long history of friendship behind us and more ahead of us. Our first meeting was on the floor of an old folks' nursing home, discovering pills hidden in the swirls of a garishly floral carpet, where we were huffing and puffing doing our antenatal exercises together, both of us expecting our first child. Sometimes we got off the floor feeling a little damp around our nether regions, worried our waters might have broken, but really we were in an old folks' home and I knew it wasn't our 'water'. Our love of France, England and travel has also bound us together along with food, cooking and colour. Our husbands are on the periphery but take a role in our many fun times together, be that pouring drinks or driving us around. There must be something else...?

Dave and Ginny were already at Rebecca's, having arrived that morning from London, and would be at the house to greet us. It was the most glorious day, with sapphire-blue skies and bright, dazzling sunshine. Steve and I were in a great holiday and festive mood and I was excited to be going away. As we came over a rise on the motorway, we could see the magnificent Pyrenees sitting so majestically and clearly on the horizon. The peaks, covered in crisp white snow, sparkled like thousands of tiny diamonds in the sun. It was a breathtaking sight.

An hour into our journey, I nudged Steve. 'Time for coffee, please. Can we pull in soon?'

'Yep, I could do with one, too.'

A mile on from the magnificent Carcassonne fortress, we stopped at one of the many large motorway service stations (called *aires* in France), which always have a café, mini supermarket, toilet facilities and often restaurants. Some even have camping grounds and others are just a place to pull in and have a rest. We stood at the café counter to stretch our legs and drink our coffee. This particular stop offered a wine shop, too, filled with regional choices. We bought a couple of bottles to add to our and Rebecca's Christmas stash.

The front door was thrown open as soon as we pulled up outside Rebecca's home. There Ginny stood, with a huge smile and a frosty, fizzing glass of champagne in each hand.

'*Bonjour*, Annemarie and Steve,' she chirped. 'Merry Christmas!'

'Merry Christmas!' we sang back, hauling bags, wine and gifts out of the boot of the car. Quickly dumping them inside the front door, we took the proffered glasses from Ginny.

Dave and Rebecca materialised behind her, beaming, with their and Ginny's glass of champagne. What a wonderful greeting and a delicious way to start our Christmas together. We stood chatting in the garden in the winter sunshine, catching up on all the news before moving inside to unpack everything.

Rebecca is very particular and fussy in her kitchen, as most professionals are, so as soon as we stepped foot inside the door all of us were barred from it, not allowed to help with any food preparation or to wash a dish. This seemed so rude to Ginny and me as both of us are hands-on in the kitchen and used to mucking in.

'Are you sure I can't help you, Rebecca?' I offered, once we'd stowed our bags in our room.

Ginny, sitting on the sofa, waved her hand, dismissing me and giving Rebecca a resigned grin at the same time.

'Don't even bother to ask, Annemarie. She won't let us near the kitchen.'

'Dave and I can do the dishes at least,' Steve pathetically offered, winking at Dave.

'Don't go volunteering me for any duties, thanks very much,' Dave spluttered. 'She won't let you near. You won't know where anything goes and, besides, Rebecca's worried you might break something.' It was Dave's turn to wink at Rebecca.

'Look, you people, I prefer to do things *my* way in the kitchen and to put everything in its right place. Then I know exactly where it is when I'm looking for it,' Rebecca countered primly. 'It's very nice of you to offer, but no, thank you. That's settled. We'll hear no more about it.' She slapped the arm of her chair to reinforce her words. Rebecca had a very determined look on her face so no one said another thing. We let her get on with making it a real holiday for the rest of us.

The day we arrived, there had been a debate about whether we should have a Christmas tree or not. Dave was adamant we needed one. He jumped to his feet.

'Come on, you lot. We're going to find a Christmas tree this afternoon. Christmas just isn't Christmas without a tree. We'll need decorations, too. Hurry up,' he yelled, snatching the car keys off the table and grabbing his jacket.

Steve, Ginny and I leapt up, scrabbled for our coats and hats and headed for the door. After several fruitless stops, we found the perfect tree, according to Dave the Oracle. The boys stuffed it in through the boot, between Ginny and me in the backseat. Both of us held the branches down so we could talk over the top of it; don't worry, we managed perfectly well. Back at Rebecca's, the afternoon quickly darkened into a blue-black, frosty evening. Steve organised and poured the drinks; Rebecca plated up some delicious nibbles and Dave and Ginny decorated our gorgeous Christmas tree. I sat back on the sofa like the queen and enjoyed it all. A perfect day.

The next afternoon the four of us got ourselves kitted up in hats, gloves and jackets. We needed to walk a few kilometres to make room for yet more food and give Rebecca a bit of quiet time. It was Christmas Eve and after our walk we drove into the historic, walled town of Aigue-Mortes for a drink in the square. It was bitterly cold. There looked to be mainly locals out with only a few foreigners like us.

'Come on, Annemarie. Let's look in some of the shops. The boys can have a beer and a chat and wait for us.' Ginny took my arm.

'Don't hurry back, girls,' Steve called after us. 'We'll be just fine,' he said, looking to Dave for backup.

'Yes, yes. You take your time. No rush.' Dave smirked.

Honestly, they were like a couple of silly schoolboys. We knew they'd slip in a second beer before we returned to Rebecca's.

On the way back, we stopped at the local McDonald's to log into the wifi and pick up our emails as there was no internet at Rebecca's. Our inbox was overflowing with Christmas messages from family and friends. My heart cracked a little reading these and I dissolved into tears. Ginny, arriving back from the loo, put her arm around me.

'Oh no, what on earth's happened, Annemarie? D'you have bad news? Tell me.'

'No, no, it's just me being pathetic,' I blubbered. 'Take no notice. I'm just finding it a bit difficult, not being with our boys. I'll be fine. Just give me a minute.' I pulled my tissues out and mopped up.

'It's the same for us with our two.' Ginny slumped for a moment then rallied. 'It's always this time of year you miss those you can't be with. They'll have a great day and d'you know what? So will we,' she said decisively.

In Auckland, Christmas family lunch was usually at our home where 15 or more of us would sit down, tucking into sides of roasted salmon, beef eye fillet, ham on the bone, roast potatoes with all the trimmings and plenty of salads. We always set up two long tables in our front courtyard, sheltered from the burning sun by the canopy and umbrellas. Lunch would gradually drift to an end in the late afternoon when friends would pop in. Festivities would be resumed, the barbecue lit, salads refreshed and we'd continue well into the night. I was happy, though, knowing Archie and Callum were together with family and close friends and we were with Dave, Ginny and Rebecca. Our sons ended up having a wonderful time and so did we, even though 12,000 miles separated us.

Ever since the boys were toddlers, I'd filled a Christmas stocking and left it hanging on their bedroom door. When they woke on Christmas morning, we would hear their excitement from our bedroom. I kept the tradition going, even though they were now men. But how was I going to do that from the other side of the world? I enlisted the secretive help of Archie's girlfriend who put stockings together for me, stuffing them with socks, undies, toiletries and sweets. In late November I also sent Callum, Archie and his girlfriend an Advent calendar, filled with chocolates, another childhood tradition I wanted to continue. I didn't think about Archie living in Adelaide's 35-degree heat. The result—a melted mess in the letterbox.

One year when our sons were little, there was a great drama. We'd given each of the boys an Advent calendar and they knew the rules of opening one window a day. The very next day, the thumping and yelling from Callum's bedroom soon let me know there was a problem. I ran down the stairs.

'What on earth's going on, you two? Stop it right now!' I glared at both of them. 'Right, Archie, tell me what's happened,' I said, holding each boy by the arm, keeping them apart.

'Callum's opened every window in my Advent calendar and eaten all the chocolate,' Archie wailed.

I took a look. Each little window had been very carefully closed to appear as though it was still intact.

'Did you, Callum?'

A rather sheepish and sorry-looking Callum mumbled, 'Yeees.'

'What do you say to Archie, Callum?' I asked sternly.

'Sorry, Archie,' he whispered, looking downcast.

'Right, well I think the decent thing to do, Callum, is to give Archie your calendar. You've eaten all his chocolate so he deserves to have yours. Give it to him now and that's the end of it,' I said.

Callum reluctantly handed the calendar over and Archie hurried to his room to hide it.

❋ ❋ ❋

During our stay, beautiful food appeared on the table at every mealtime. We felt like royalty. Several afternoons we left Rebecca having a little snooze in her favourite chair in the sitting room.

'You don't think she'll mind us slipping out without her?' I whispered to Dave and Ginny, shutting the front door as quietly as possible so as not to disturb her and tiptoeing to the car.

'Absolutely not. Rebecca needs to keep her strength up,' Dave insisted once we were in the car. 'Given the amount of cooking and washing up she's got to do,' he said, laughing heartily as his joke.

'Dave!' Ginny slapped his arm. 'That's not funny.' She was quietly laughing, too.

'Well, it's true,' he countered. 'She won't let us help at all.'

What a Christmas Day. Rebecca prepared an enormous feast and we started with canapés and champagne around 1 p.m., after the arrival of three of Rebecca's friends from London. The first course followed, as did the second, then the third, then the fourth. After a hugely convivial meal and much hilarity, we staggered from the table around 7 p.m. Each course was outstanding. The drink got the better of us so no one realised that dessert was still sitting in the kitchen. No matter, we couldn't have fitted it in anyway so took it to another get-together on Boxing Day.

At the end of our stay, we kissed Rebecca goodbye at the gate, thanking her for such a wonderful Christmas. She'd been amazing. I'm sure she went to lie down for the rest of the day.

19

Introductions

'I'm tickled pink you're coming to stay, Gin.' I grinned at her sitting across from me in the back seat. 'You and Dave will be our first guests. I hope you get to meet Mary and Symon so you can see for yourselves how nice they are. This afternoon, though, I thought we might go over and have a cuppa with Siobhan and Doug? Afterwards we could take a sneaky look at Mas de Lavande, where we used to work. There's no one there at the moment, according to Siobhan. What d'you think?'

'We'd love to meet them all, of course. I'm looking forward to it. I feel as if I know them already from everything you've told me.' She smiled. 'And yes, let's go over to Brens. Apart from seeing where you worked, it would be good to have a trip around this area. I've looked it up online and it looks beautiful.'

'Well, we think it's gorgeous. Perhaps it's not as appealing right now as it is in the summer but autumn and winter have their own beauty, don't you think? I'm loving experiencing the seasons here,' I replied.

As we arrived in Gaillac, we came up the hill to 'our place'. To me the house looked very impressive through the leafless poplars lining the drive. When all the trees were in full leaf in summer, the house was partially hidden from view. In winter, the pale-pink stone and multi-paned and shuttered windows were even more striking. The terracotta-tiled roof and tall *pigeonnier* stood out against the stark vineyard backdrop. It was such a beautiful property.

'Oh yes, very gorgeous,' admired Ginny as we turned in the gates. Dave gave a low whistle. 'That's one beautiful house.'

In the cottage, and after a quick unpack and a look around, Ginny arrived back in the kitchen. Putting the kettle on, she turned to me.

'Get me the floor plan for this place please. Honestly, Annemarie, this is all Dave and I need.' She waved her arms to take in the space. 'Adding a small storage area under the stairs would be handy if this was your permanent home. But really, this is just fantastic.'

And it was. We were so comfortable living there. There was plenty of space for the two of us plus guests. Early afternoon we drove to see Doug and Siobhan and introduced Dave and Ginny. After a quick cuppa, we continued through the forest, driving the back roads and over to Mas de Lavande where we'd experienced our first and subsequently disastrous foray into living and working in France. It was a lovely surprise to notice Gabriel turn into the driveway 30 seconds before us. It was so good to see him again, chat and to introduce him to our friends. Gabriel and Steve wandered off to the garden together so Steve could see how it was all looking.

As Dave peered through the windows of the cottage we'd occupied, he snorted. 'Well there's no comparison, is there? Your new home is a palace compared to this. How on earth did you live here?'

How very true, in every sense. Now that we were at Combe de Merigot, it was hard for me to imagine that I'd ever lived at Mas de Lavande. I guess we'd just made the best of it. Nothing had changed. There were still the ramshackle chairs and table and the worn, old, wicker bedspread still lay over the back of the couch. So all the promises made of new furniture and furnishings never eventuated. I wasn't surprised, given what went on while we worked there. It all looked so seedy and uncared for. At least we'd cleaned it from top to bottom to make it habitable for us.

Late afternoon when we were back home, almost on cue Symon and Mary called us over to have a drink. They'd seen us arrive and wanted to meet our friends. Anne and Bruno, who owned Domaine Duffau, the vineyard at the bottom of our road, were there, too. It turned into a fun and noisy evening with all of us around the fire in the gorgeous drawing room. Dinner back in our cottage was rather late that night. *Did we even have dinner, Steve? I don't remember…*

Doug and Siobhan were booked to have a meal with the four of us the next evening so I invited Mary and Symon to come for a drink and was so glad I did. We ended up having canapés and the delicious champagne they'd given us for Christmas, plus another bottle that Gin and Dave brought with them. Let's just say it was a lively evening with the eight of us in our tiny living room.

After our Christmas sojourn, Steve and I needed to get a few jobs done so Dave and Ginny were going to take our car the following day and head to Albi to go sightseeing.

'Steve, where's the best place to park?' Dave asked after breakfast, plonking his empty coffee cup in the sink. 'Let's find it in your GPS. That'll save a lot of hassle and wasted time.'

The two boys sorted the plans while Ginny got herself ready upstairs.

'Make sure you go into the cathedral as it's stunning. The ceiling is something else.' I was lounging in the armchair chatting while Ginny rubbed moisturiser into her face. 'Also, the covered market in the centre is a visual feast. You'll be able to have a delicious lunch, too. There're lots of lovely cafés and restaurants to choose from. We don't need the car so take your time and enjoy everything. See you back here for a glass of rosé late afternoon.'

'I'm sure we'll find somewhere delicious to eat. Thanks for all the info and the car,' Ginny responded.

I got up, hugged her goodbye and headed down the stairs and across the drive to the house.

Our short time with Ginny and Dave came to an end when Steve dropped them off at Toulouse train station the next day. It was easy to say goodbye as we'd arranged for Ginny to come back for a few days mid-January. 'Our' family would have returned to London and New York by then. There would be time for Ginny and me to go exploring and perhaps get into the gorgeous boutiques of Toulouse.

20

A New Year

Happy New Year! It was 7:30 a.m. on the first day of January. My great need for a cup of tea got me out of bed, even though we didn't climb into it until after 1 a.m. It was pitch black outside so I had no idea what sort of day it was. Daylight didn't usually arrive until around 8:15 a.m. and, anyway, it didn't matter. Mary and Symon didn't need me and Steve wouldn't be doing an airport run until later in the morning.

Our New Year's Eve had begun at 7:30 a.m. as it was 8:30 p.m. in New Zealand. A group of friends Skyped from their dining table at one of the luxury hotels in Auckland where they were staying the night and having a New Year's Eve dinner followed by an evening of dancing.

'You all look so gorgeous,' I shouted excitedly at my laptop, sipping a cup of tea while they drank champagne. The girls were dressed in their glittery finery and the guys sported elegant jackets, shirts and trousers.

'You'll have to excuse me looking a wreck but this time difference isn't conducive to appearing at one's best.' I laughed. I was in my usual morning attire of nightie and dressing gown but did pull a brush through my hair and put some mascara on before the scheduled call. Otherwise I looked like Miss Piggy as my eyelashes are so fair. What a fright for them but they didn't care. Steve and I managed to chat with each one as we were passed around the table on Barb's iPhone. It was at those times that I really missed being with them as we always had such a lot of fun together. A little later in the morning, Steve and I caught up with our sons who sent love and messages for the New Year ahead. Bless.

I was so glad we'd accepted Mary's New Year's Eve invitation to spend it with them as it turned out to be absolutely brilliant and truly memorable.

Everyone met in the drawing room for champagne and canapés. All the young women looked wonderful in their heels and evening attire. The men were elegant, too, dressed in tailored shirts and trousers. Symon wore a tie and jacket so as soon as we walked into the kitchen and saw him so nicely dressed, I turned Steve around and pushed him back through the door. He hurried across to our cottage to grab a jacket.

The house was lovely and warm from the central heating, and the fires roaring in every fireplace gave a homely ambience. The heavy drapes shut out the dark night and cold air.

I was in charge of canapés to have with a drink and I handed around curried quail eggs tucked in endive with a tiny squirt of mayonnaise on top, smoked salmon in a dill and tabasco crème on crostini, Roquefort puffs and roasted baby tomatoes on tiny basil tarts.

Fourteen of us sat down to dinner in the winter dining room. The side lamplights added a soft ambience and Mary had dressed the table to create a winter landscape: candles flickered in red tealight holders placed along the length of the table; silver cutlery and crystal glasses gleamed in the candlelight, and woven between the tealights were fine trails of ivy and heady fronds of pine with tiny pinecones intact. My favourite, old, French-monogrammed linen napkins lay folded for each diner. As well as canapés, my other contributions to the dinner were the starter and the dessert. Red and orange balsamic-roasted beetroot (still warm), segmented oranges, toasted walnuts and goat's cheese sitting on a mixed-leaf salad bed with a Dijon mustard and orange dressing was the starter.

Symon cooked the huge haunch of beef to perfection. The accompanying dishes of Brussels sprouts and bacon, minted peas, roast parsnips and carrots tossed in honey and roasted cumin seeds were perfect. Steaming hot gravy waited on the side. Symon's fabulous red wines from the Médoc and Bordeaux flowed. The cheese board, passed around the table, groaned under the weight of a large Roquefort, a very fragrant and oozing Brie, and goat's cheese. A soft cheese covered in coffee beans was a new addition, as well as an aged Comté. The selection was outstanding.

Everyone devoured the grand finale with gusto—my hazelnut meringue filled with lemon curd folded through whipped cream, topped with more lemon curd, raspberries and a dusting of icing sugar. The chocolate roulade and raspberry coulis very quickly followed. Dinner was a great success. We got up from the table in time for a midnight countdown around the roaring fire in the foyer. Great music, fun, banter and dancing came next. It was a superb evening and one I'll always remember.

Late New Year's Day morning, Steve returned some of the young ones to the airport and the rest left in dribs and drabs during the afternoon in their hire cars. Several days later the family packed up and Steve did a run to the airport to drop them off.

Indy and Tilly settled back in with us. It was always an adjustment for them whenever the family left but they were fine after a couple of hours. Indy needed a few more cuddles and would follow us around but little Tilly took everything in her stride.

'It's time to winterise the house and gardens,' Steve announced, hanging his jacket in the laundry after his airport run. 'Symon has left me instructions on what he'd like me to do.

What's your priority?' Steve was busily pulling out a pad and pen from the desk.

'First up, change all the beds and do the laundry,' I said. 'Next will be a thorough clean of the house, top to bottom. I'll have to go up into the *pigeonnier*, too, as there'll be a carpet of dead flies up there. How they get in, I don't know as it's all sealed. I might get you to haul the vacuum cleaner up the stairs for me without whacking your head on those beams. Oh, and CH is coming in on the 5th to pack all the Christmas decorations away. Will you get the tree outside when she's done, please? The guys are coming back for it when we let them know it's ready for collection.'

'Yep, I can do all that. Just yell once CH is done. I need to get the heating on low once you've finished in the house. I'll close up all the shutters, too, except those facing the drive and road. People will then think there's someone in the house if they're looking in.' Steve put the kettle on. 'Oh, I have to go down to Mr. Bricolage hardware store to get that fleece wrap to cover the box balls and other plants in pots as well as any statuary to protect them from frost and snow. You know, that same stuff we saw at the palace in Munich. I need to drain the irrigation system as well. If the water freezes, the hoses will burst.' Steve stepped back to the table and added that to his list. 'We don't want that happening. Oh, and wrap foam around the hose leading into the taps, too.'

'What about the pool?' I closed my notebook. 'D'you have to do anything with that?'

'No, that's all good. The filter keeps the water circulating so it should be fine. But you've just reminded me. I'll need to check it.'

'Right, I might as well make a start.' I heaved myself off the couch and stretched. 'I'll get some of the linen in the wash. I might as well clean out the fridge today, too, and spray the ovens while I'm there. They'll need it after all that meat cooking at Christmas and New Year. See you later.'

Combe de Merigot would now close up for three months. Apart from the odd weekend, we wouldn't see the family until they returned for Easter at the end of March. It had been a wonderful time as the house came alive with the family at home. Every night the rooms lit up with candles or lamps, and driving up the hill in the dark of night we would see a golden glow streaming from the windows of that ancient and beautiful home.

As I stood in the laundry, loading the sheets into the machine, I thought about our life and felt so grateful for where we were living and the life we were enjoying. The upsetting news about Steve's sister being so desperately ill had given us a jolt and a reminder of just how fragile life could be. I made a silent resolution to strive for a happy and healthy year and enjoy every coming day.

21

In the Depths of Winter

At the end of January, we collected Ginny at Matabiau station in Toulouse for her second sojourn with us. While in the city, we toured through the Basilica of Saint-Sernin, enjoying the peace and incense-churchy smell inside before wandering through the vast expanse of the pink Capital square and drinking a warming hot chocolate in one of the many cafés on the perimeter. Ginny and I are both avid people-watchers so we had the perfect spot.

Our plans over the next few days, though, turned to mush, literally. Banging hard on our bedroom door, Ginny woke us the next morning as she rushed in and to the window, flinging back the curtains and shouting, 'Annemarie, Steve, wake up! It's snowing—lots. Hurry! Get up and come look.'

I sprang out of bed and joined her. The snow was falling in heavy drifts and the entire property and surrounds were a winter wonderland. The forest evergreen branches were bowed down with snow and the round, covered topiary box balls in their tubs resembled vanilla ice cream cones. The circular outside light over the side door was a white-ice bathing cap and the snowy hedges looked like an oblong cake with flicked-up frosting. We could see ice forming on the pond. It was a breathtaking sight and the air seemed almost hushed by the heavy grey/white skies. All you could hear was silence.

'It's so gorgeous.' I yawned and stretched in my PJs, marvelling at the beauty of the landscape. Dragging myself away from the view, I grabbed my dressing gown off the hook on the back of the door.

'Come on, Gin. Time for my cup of tea and your morning coffee.' I nodded towards the stairs, pushing my arms through the sleeves of the dressing gown and scuffing down in my slippers to the kitchen. We left Steve dozing in bed for a little longer. Ten minutes later he arrived in the doorway. Seeing Steve's attire (or lack of it), Ginny and I were taken aback for a few seconds then started laughing.

'What on earth are you doing, Steve?' I stared in disbelief at what he was wearing. 'It's snowing and freezing outside.'

He'd donned his new stubbies and the woollen socks our friend Ann had sent him from New Zealand but he was bare-chested. He just grinned at us, not saying a word, and made for the back door. Tilly and Indy squeezed past to beat him outside.

Good God, Steve had lost the plot. I picked up my phone to get a photo of him prancing around the garden topless in the pristine snow, while it was snowing. The fool. Ginny and I were giggling like schoolgirls.

'You two have been living in the countryside too long, Annemarie. Steve's gone completely bonkers.' Ginny chuckled.

'I think he must have.' I rolled my eyes and pulled a silly face at him through the glass.

Steve in his stubbies

Indy leapt around Steve, barking and barking, totally bewildered by his antics and trying to catch the snow in her mouth. Tilly was also going a little mad. She was hilarious as she jumped about like a kangaroo, yelping and biting bits of snow and ice.

I posted a photo on my blog of Steve clowning around in the snow. Our email pinged not long afterwards. It was our friend Andy in London, sending a photo of himself doing the same thing with his dog in their snow-covered garden. He'd tagged his email with 'anything Steve can do… (I can do better)'.

The three of us were drawn to the windows most of the morning, fascinated by the falling snow. It was the first time for us to experience snow like that. Yes, we saw it in Munich but it had melted away fairly quickly. Here it was getting very deep.

I'd booked the Michelin-starred restaurant La Falaise in Cahuzac-sur-Vère for lunch that day as a little treat in Ginny's honour. We were all looking forward to it but the snow was piling up fast and still falling. Any attempt to get to the restaurant would have to be in the Range Rover and even then I didn't know if we'd make it.

'I don't think we should go to Cahuzac for lunch today,' I ventured. 'Sorry to be a party pooper but I think it's going to be dangerous. There's quite a climb up to the village from the main road and it will be very icy and slippery. Before we even *get* to the main road, we have to negotiate our drive and the hill down.'

Steve was keen to give it a go but I was glad Ginny was pragmatic.

'No, it's not worth the risk. What if we get stuck? I know someone would come and rescue us but there's no point. I agree, Annemarie. I think we should stay put.'

'To be honest, I would be nervous and upset if we dented Symon's Range Rover, sliding into something. I'm going to give the restaurant a call and cancel lunch.' I picked up my phone and rang.

It was such a shame but we would have been very foolish to attempt to drive in that weather.

When the snow started melting two days later, our pond filled to the top edge of the bank. A beautiful, short-stay visitor arrived—a white heron. It would perch in the trees for a brief time and then gracefully glide down, turning in figures of eight before landing and promenading around the lake's edge, no doubt looking for fish.

Late one glorious morning, the roads were clear and safer so Ginny and I went out for a jaunt to Puycelsi and Bruniquel. Being winter, the villages were deserted but we enjoyed our little excursion and hot coffee in the warm Puycelsi café with some of the locals.

Our few days with Ginny were relaxing, deep in snow, playing Scrabble, reading and watching TV. Steve managed to get Ginny safely up the icy drive in the Range Rover and to the airport for her London flight. She may have been worried she might be stuck with us and our quiet, sedate life for a few more days.

According to friends in the area, January and February were notorious for being the cold and quiet months. People hunkered down and didn't do much but we were still waiting to get lonely or bored. We'd been getting to know the French neighbours during this time. Robert and Nicole, in their 60s, lived directly across the road from Combe de Merigot. I met Robert for the first time at the top of our drive after the heavy snow. Both of us were inspecting the road to see if we could get out.

I called out a cheery, *'Bonjour, la neige est très jolie, oui?'* (Hello, the snow is very pretty, yes?) He crossed the road to speak to me and I felt like I'd been hit by machine-gun fire as he let off a few sentences in the local dialect at a hundred kilometres an hour and I had no clue what he was saying. I explained that my French wasn't very good but my husband spoke it and we were New Zealanders. One thing I managed to catch in the next burst was huuuurgby. Translated—rugby. Toulouse is a strong rugby city and everyone knows New Zealand for the All Blacks' prowess. Thank goodness Steve arrived up the drive and took over from me. Robert and Nicole came for an apéritif one night in January, followed a week later by Clothilde and Olivier, the parents of Lazarus, the now-dead chicken.

During December, Bruno and Ann, the winemakers and owners of Domaine Duffau, had come for drinks and dinner. They were great fun, well-travelled and French, but spoke perfect English which made my life a whole lot easier. Our friend Barb had very kindly sent me a delicious bottle of New Zealand Sauvignon Blanc and Bruno savoured every drop of the two glasses I poured him.

'Ah, Annemarie, I do wish I could make wine like this,' he sighed, holding his glass up to the light and admiring the wine's almost imperceptible pale-green tinge. He then put his nose into the glass. 'This is so floral and fruity. Alas, wine is all about the *terroir* (a particular region's climate, soil and terrain that affects wine taste). In Gaillac the *terroir* is so very different to that in New Zealand.'

Late January, Bruno and Ann returned our hospitality and invited us for dinner. Clothilde and Olivier came too and a gorgeous, young Frenchman (another winemaker) whose family vineyard was only five kilometres from Combe de Merigot. He'd spent a year in the vineyards of Cromwell in New Zealand which he'd loved and we were able to have a good chat about Central Otago Pinot Noir, the people and the countryside.

Bruno was very proud to announce dinner.

'Annemarie, Steve, have you eaten *choucroute* before?' Bruno placed heavily laden plates down in front of us. 'It's a specialty of Alsace.'

'No, Bruno, we haven't. Sounds, um, delicious, but what is it exactly?' I leant over my plate, examining it all. I should have remembered that the now-French Alsace region has, over the centuries, been repeatedly invaded by the Germans. A lot of the cuisine from those times has remained.

The *choucroute* consisted of two different types of sausage, a slab of fatty bacon, loads of sauerkraut and potatoes. The realisation dawned as to why those German men we met in the Munich Hofbräuhaus were so big and brawny. I furtively slipped Steve the potato, politely declined the bacon and slowly chewed my way through the rest. It was such a dense, heavy dinner with the cheese that followed then the pavlova I'd made. I only ate slivers of the cheese and pavlova, but still I was clutching my protruding stomach and groaning on the drive back up the hill to our place. The thing I most enjoyed was the delicious dessert wine Bruno made which complemented the pavlova beautifully. We would be returning to buy some once it was bottled. His 'bubbles' too were delicious and he gave us a bottle to open on a special occasion.

22

The Hills are Alive

Time was rushing by and already it was February. I'd come in from walking the dogs and was thawing out on the couch with a cup of hot tea. It was 3°C but with the wind in my face coming up the hill, it felt positively arctic and my pink cheeks were stinging. My new possum and merino scarf and hat, a gift from my sister Marilyn, kept me snug and warm, as did the pair of fur-trimmed merino gloves some of our tennis club crowd had given me.

I'd just celebrated a mid-50s birthday. I still felt like 40 but looking in the mirror told the real story. Not much I could do about that. I was alive and well and finally living my dream. Who could ask for more? Certainly not me. I was spoilt with presents and cards from home and emails from family and friends. Denise cooked a memorable and delicious dinner at her home a few nights later—a Delia Smith oven-roasted porcini risotto. It was so good.

On the day of my birthday, Steve and I were at the Conti for our usual coffee and a *pain aux raisins*, stopping to pick up a few things at Leclerc supermarket on the way back. We bumped into Siobhan and Doug coming out.

'Hello, you two. How are you both?' I was so pleased to see them. We exchanged kisses and pleasantries for a minute.

'Doug fancies McDonald's for lunch.' Siobhan raised her eyebrows at us. 'I don't suppose that would be on your normal lunch menu but d'you fancy joining us?'

I looked at Steve and hoped he'd read my mind as I willed him not to mention my birthday. I didn't want a fuss or have them feel compelled to say the obligatory Happy Birthday.

'Annemarie? I fancy McDonald's; how about you?' Steve checked with me. I don't think I've ever eaten a birthday lunch in McDonald's but I knew Steve would love his first burger and fries in over a year.

'Sure, we'd love to.' It was a novelty, that's for sure, but very enjoyable to spend my birthday with Siobhan and Doug.

I chose to have my proper birthday celebration at La Falaise, the Michelin-starred restaurant I'd cancelled when Ginny was with us. We'd previously attempted to have lunch there one beautiful, sunny Sunday but arriving at the door without a booking wasn't sensible as there wasn't one empty table.

'Not to worry. While we're here, I'll book for the night of your actual birthday.' Steve was at reception, finding the date with the girl on the desk.

It felt so nice to dress up the night we eventually went and to put on heels and wear makeup.

'Where's Steve gone?' I teased before we went out that night, looking over the shoulder of the man standing in front of me. Steve looked very smart in a dress shirt and good trousers instead of his usual stubbies and T-shirt. I just got a snort in response. 'Ooh, it's like having a date with a new man.' I winked at him. 'I'm looking forward to this.'

'Get in the car, woman, and stop your blathering,' he said, pretending to be cross and giving me a nudge through the door.

We arrived at 7:30 p.m. and were the first. We sat down, thumbing through the menu, sipping a glass of champagne.

When 8 p.m. came and still no one else had arrived, I didn't think too much of it as this was France and people did eat late. We ordered and partway through our first course, I again looked around. There were no other guests in the restaurant.

'Excuse me,' I said to the waiter. 'What time do most people book dinner for?'

'Now, *madame*,' he replied politely.

'Well, where is everyone?' The waiter's eyes followed mine around the room.

'There's no one else, *madame*. You're the only booking this evening,' he said, deadpan.

We were taken aback. Fancy opening the restaurant for only one booking. It was a Tuesday night and the waiter said that the restaurant was really only busy Friday and Saturday evening and Sunday lunchtime during winter.

As part of the main course, there was a cube of jellied pâté on my plate. It was delicious. When the waiter came to clear our plates, I asked him what that pâté was. Once I discovered it was made from parts of the head and feet of a pig, a thick lump rose up and almost closed my throat. I swallowed hard and drank a glass of water, praying the food would stay down. I was glad I didn't know beforehand.

We planned to return one Sunday lunchtime when there would be more atmosphere with a room full of diners. Lunchtime was always a lot cheaper, too.

Four days of continuous golden sunshine in March woke the countryside from its sleepy winter hibernation and brought it to life again. Smoke trails dribbled across the sky as vintners burnt off the vine prunings and locals made the most of the brilliant days. Both Robert and Olivier were out rotary-hoeing their vegetable patches, getting ready for the spring planting.

Steve, too, was busy, digging over our little kitchen garden and the house garden, adding in mountains of horse manure and covering it with straw. Cyclists were either flying down our hill or huffing and puffing up it, and walkers, poles in hand, strode across the fields below us. Everywhere we went, people smiled, marvelling at seeing the sun, the temperature being a little warmer and how it was reviving us all. It most definitely was.

Alas, we all spoke too soon as the good weather didn't last and we found ourselves in the throes of early-spring, gale-force winds.

'I've never known wind like this, Steve.' The door slammed shut behind me, caught in a frenzied blast while I pushed the hair back out of my face.

'It's crazy alright. The entire driveway is strewn with branches and even some of the bigger ones are down. I'll take the 4x4 to clear them once it lets up a bit.' Steve was at the desk.

'The sheets were either wrapped around the clothesline or heading for the vines. I've given up and they're now in the dryer. What a fight!' I slumped into the nearest chair. 'Have you looked at the forecast? How long have we got these winds? Three days of this is doing my head in,' I moaned. 'I have great sympathy for those in Provence who suffer those mistral winds for weeks on end.'

'Yep I did and you've only got to put up with it for another day.' Steve closed the weather window on his laptop. 'Should be done and dusted by Thursday.'

'Thank heavens for that.' I got up to put the kettle on for a much-needed cup of tea.

Our social life was well and truly on the up, thanks to Sarah. She emailed me about the cancer charity evening we'd been invited to.

So good you're coming to the fundraiser. Apart from the donation going to a good cause, it's always a great evening. You'll be able to meet more people, too. One couple in particular is great fun—Ruth and Malcolm. I know you'll get on well with them. Richard and I'll swing by Merigot and pick you up. No point in taking two cars. Oh and it's smart dress but you don't need to worry; no one dresses up too smartly. See you Saturday. xx

Steve and I had already learnt the hard way about the dress code when we had our first outing with Siobhan and Doug while working at Mas de Lavande. We'd attended a quiz night, dressing up in nicer clothes than usual. Both of us stood out like sore thumbs and were obviously foreigners.

The guests at the fundraiser were mainly French and lots of nodding, handshakes and *bonsoirs* were exchanged around the room. Everyone sat down to a delicious four-course meal. The entire meal cost €5 per person and that included wine. We couldn't believe it. There was something very wrong there. They could have charged €10 a head and still it wouldn't have covered the cost of the food so we guessed it was donated. The committee produced an excellent evening with skits performed by various groups. Even better, we were delighted to find that Malcolm and Ruth were outgoing, a lot of fun and very natural. We really enjoyed their company and that evening was the start of our ongoing friendship.

They rang several days later and asked us over for coffee and, subsequently, for supper. Nowadays, New Zealanders call supper 'dinner'. In my teens, supper to us was a cup of tea and a biscuit *after* dinner. Also in that era in New Zealand, dinner would be eaten anywhere between 6 and 7 p.m. at the latest. We discovered what supper was to some English people the hard way, 30 years earlier. I have to tell you the story as it still makes me smile when I remember it. Andy and Emma, the friends we'd spent a fabulous week with in a Tuscan villa they rented, lived in

London. When I was about 24 or 25, they came on transfer to live and work in New Zealand for a couple of years. Andy and I worked together in the corporate team of Barclays Bank in Wellington. They invited us for supper at 8 p.m. one Saturday night.

That evening, Steve and I ate dinner at home, duly arriving at their place at 8 p.m. Unbeknown to us, Emma had been hard at work in the kitchen and produced the most fabulous three-course meal. What idiots we were. Steve and I exchanged discreetly raised eyebrows and politely waded our way through it all, clutching our bloated stomachs in the car on the way home. We confessed to them some months later and we've laughed about it with them for years since.

Anyway, we were looking forward to having *supper* with our new friends Ruth and Malcolm and their friends. There would definitely not be any food consumed beforehand.

As time went on, we came to know Ruth and Malc well and spent lots of quality time with them. They'd both lived in the same UK village but met for the first time at a party given by mutual friends. Ruth was an IT project manager in the City, working in the investment sector, and Malc was with the London Fire Brigade, joining up when he was 18 years old. They came to live in Cahuzac-sur-Vere after a long, liquid lunch in London where they pulled up a map of France and Ruth closed her eyes and stuck a wobbly finger on it. Decision made. They would be buying a place in the Tarn department in the Occitanie region of Southern France and moved to their derelict barn in 2002 when Ruth was made redundant. They renovated it as and when time and money permitted and had created a lovely, welcoming home. Malc commuted to London for ten years until he retired and took up gardening and maintenance for people in the area.

As well as helping Malc with his bits and pieces, Ruth began catering for locals and we discovered she'd even catered for Mary and Symon and the family while they were having renovations done at Combe de Merigot.

They're both dog mad and if Ruth were to choose, it would be dogs over humans. If there's no space on the sofa because the dogs are on it, well, tough luck, you'll be standing for the evening. Not quite, but something close to it. When we met them, they owned three beautiful creatures: Luna, a black Labrador, Sirius, a black setter and Gus, a black Rottweiler/Labrador. On our first visit, it was terrifying to arrive to arrive and knock on their door. The barking and howling that went on behind it engendered great fear of what would happen once the door opened. Malc would be holding one dog by the collar and the other two with his knees while we were kissed and welcomed in, squeezing our way past the dogs. They recognised you were friend not foe and by the end of the evening we would be covered in slobber with the dogs having smothered us in love. It happened every time we knocked.

A few nights after the cancer charity fundraiser, I ended up sitting in candlelight in our living room. No, it wasn't a romantic evening with my husband, because he wasn't there. He'd made a last-minute dash to New Zealand for a week to have time with Margot. I was caught in the middle of a power cut and getting quite antsy about how long the electricity would be off. I felt very alone for the first time since leaving New Zealand. Not lonely, just alone as Mary and Symon were back in London. Steve and I always left a light on in the cottage to find our way around in the night should we need to come downstairs. It was pitch black in the countryside and we couldn't see a foot in front of us. It was sod's law that the first time we'd had a power cut, Steve happened to be away. I was all alone, in the cottage, down a long drive, off the main road, in the countryside…

'Stop it, you stupid girl,' I chided myself. I was pretty spooked but having the dogs in the house did give me a little comfort. I took myself off to bed early, lying under the covers, peering over the top of the duvet into the black night, and prayed the power would be back on soon.

Margot was very ill and enduring many tests, treatments and operations on her broken bones. She'd broken both arms and one shoulder needed total reconstruction. She was also undergoing intense chemo. The long-term prognosis was grim and Simon had suggested Steve return sooner rather than later. Her attitude, fortitude and inner strength during all this was incredible. The family was in awe of how she dealt with her illness considering her intense pain and discomfort.

She was thrilled to see Steve and he was so pleased he'd made the effort to fly back to be with her. When our sons discovered he was heading to New Zealand, they both organised to be with him and it turned into a tremendous social whirl. Steve and one of the boys stayed with friends, Ann and Kevin, and they got to see our extended family as well. I found it strange, sitting in Southwest France, knowing my family was all together without me. Their fun time, though, was tinged with the worry and sadness of what Margot was suffering.

I kept busy with dog walking and domestics and went to movies and dinners with friends. Ginny kept in touch, Skyping most days, but I was just fine and apart from the night without power, I was enjoying having space to myself for the first time in a while.

One beautiful, warm and sunny morning after running errands in Gaillac, I sat daydreaming and enjoying a coffee on the front terrace of the Conti. While savouring the drink and warmed by the sun on my face, I realised just how much I liked the slower and more contented pace of life, having both English and French friends and being able to immerse ourselves fully into French life. There was also that guilty thought—why was I so fortunate and Margot so dreadfully ill? There was no answer.

One of my five sisters, Marilyn, was due to arrive with her partner, Tony, and I was so looking forward to having them stay. Down by the lake, the pussy willow was coming into blossom and on the large expanse of lawn, pretty, tiny purple and white crocuses were poking their heads through and citrus-green leaves were emerging on the trees.

Wild, spicy chives sprouted in the lawn and I would use these in salads and salmon dishes. From the top floor of the house, I could see the foragers out, searching the roadside banks and ditches for the thin wild asparagus that grew there. All of these new-life awakenings heralded spring was just around the corner and it felt like anything was possible.

Ducks arrived on our pond, sending Indy into a frenzy trying to catch them. No such luck. All she got was a cacophony of quacks and squawks and sent them into the middle of the pond with her barking. It drove her nuts not being able to get at them. The days were becoming longer and maybe, just maybe, we would have a stunning summer.

Steve flew direct both ways to New Zealand and France and was soon back 'in the French zone' after one night's good sleep. I drooled as he pulled the old, familiar New Zealand goodies out of his suitcase—Vegemite, Vogel's bread, Mainland Tasty Cheddar Cheese, pineapple chunks and Cadbury's Fruit & Nut bars. Next came Whittaker's Peanut Slabs and three bottles of sauvignon blanc. Woo hoo!

'What are you doing?' Steve leant over my shoulder as I put a slice of Vogel's bread into the toaster.

'What d'you think I'm doing? I haven't eaten Vogel's toast for over a year.' I began slathering the now popped-up toast in butter and Vegemite. 'I'm going to enjoy this.' I took a huge, greedy bite. 'Oh I've missed this so much.' I closed my eyes while munching away to savour it that little bit more. 'Sorry to speak with my mouth full but it's so delicious.'

'Ann thought I was mad bringing wine and cheese to France,' Steve chuckled, 'but I know you love our sauvignon blanc.' He began putting our lovely treats away in the kitchen cupboards, and the now-empty suitcase stood at the bottom of the stairs, waiting until he went up.

Licking the last of the butter and Vegemite off my fingers, I said, 'Yes, it's a bit daft, I know, but I'm so glad you did.'

23

Easter Feasts and Medical Misadventures

Mary and Symon returned for Easter, bringing friends with them. The week before, we opened the house up properly again, flinging windows open each fine day to let the breeze through and doing a dust and another vacuum. Don't ask me how those pesky flies got into a closed-up house, but they did, batches of them lying dead on windowsills. I did a run to Le Clerc with a huge shopping list and spent a day in the kitchen, getting food prep done. I cooked for everyone on Easter Thursday and Good Friday nights then Steve and I were free as birds as Mary and Symon were taking care of themselves and their friends for the rest of the weekend. Once again we were thoroughly spoilt by them with champagne and chocolates. Just a little Easter gift, you realise. I got fatter after each visit.

On the Saturday, Steve and I made the most of the family being around to care for the dogs and drove down to Castres for the day, an hour away, as I wanted to check out the Goya Museum. It was pouring with rain but often breaking into patches of sunshine and once parked, we ducked and dived to keep dry. Castres is a pretty town with colourful, old houses which date from the Middle Ages perched along the edge of the Agoût River. In the 17th century, they were occupied by tanners, weavers and dyers who put Castres on the map as a top textile centre. These houses were built on large, stone cellars with doors that opened directly over the water.

The Goya Museum is relatively small but perfectly formed with its exquisite parquet floors and intricate, wrought-iron railing and curved stone staircase. It holds the most extensive collection of Spanish paintings in France. An exhibition, very reminiscent of Picasso's work, was on in one of the galleries. I've never really liked much of Picasso's stuff as to my untrained eye, some of his creations have a very twisted and tortured look, which was exactly what I was seeing. I was taken with the building as well as some of Goya's and other artists' work. The museum shares space with the Cathédrale Saint-Benoît de Castres which is stunning with its intricate, gold and blue vaulted ceilings and detailed statuary. The deeply carved pulpit sits at the top of an ornate and curved timber staircase high up above the congregation. Back in the day, I guess this gave the minister a sense of domination to instil fear in the parishioners. France has some incredible, little-known cathedrals and churches, and this is one of them.

Easter Sunday lunch at Ruth and Malcolm's left me on the couch in the recovery position. Steve and I had eaten our way through a four-course feast, having a wonderful time with them and their guests. Ruth and Malc are very social beasts and there was always a crowd at their place. When we arrived home from lunch at 5:30 p.m., I lay down, holding my full tummy and groaning aloud. At 7:15 p.m. Steve rolled me off the couch and we were out of the door again, this time to Denise and Ian's for another marathon session of four courses. Talk about gluttons for punishment—do pardon the pun. We so wanted to be at both events but, in hindsight, I should have said no to a course or two.

※ ※ ※

Finally Steve and I were both registered in the French medical system. Fundamental to getting our *carte Vitale* was the necessity to have our birth and marriage certificates translated into French by an authorised agent and submitted to the authorities which took an inordinate amount of time to get done.

We'd registered with a medical practice in Gaillac—the Drs Chalan, a French husband and wife team recommended by Denise. Both spoke a little English, although hers was better than his. I'd somehow severely twisted my back, could hardly walk and the pain was intense. Steve whizzed me down in the car to the doctors' surgery, with me yelping in pain on every bump he went over. I couldn't get comfortable at all. It was just awful.

My appointment was with Mr/Dr Chalan, who was very thorough and gave me an injection in my bottom to give immediate pain relief. My God, the sting from the jab caused me *more* pain for the first ten minutes. It was so deep, intense and excruciating, I hobbled around the surgery whimpering, with tears streaming down my face. After a week of medication and rest when I could, my back slowly came right. With the amount of bed-making I did, it needed to be fixed.

I booked a return visit to see the doctor as I wanted a referral to visit an osteopath to get some proper work done on my back. This time I saw Mrs/Dr Chalan who was also extremely thorough. She sent me for full blood tests and gave me a slip to get a bone density test done. In France if you want to do any physical activity, such as yoga, join a gym or play sport, you have to provide a clearance letter from your doctor. On a practical level, all the letter states is that your blood pressure and heart are fine. That's if they are, of course. I wanted to attend a keep-fit class so the doctor gave me a letter for this, too. I was very impressed with Mrs/Dr Chalan.

A few months on, it was time for me to have my annual physical check-ups—a mammogram and smear test. What a vastly different experience these were compared to those done in Auckland.

'How did you get on?' Steve asked when I walked through the door late one afternoon, feeling a little flummoxed from the check-ups.

'Well, where do I begin? It was certainly different. When she asked me to remove my lower clothing, I did so, looking for the sheet to cover myself. There wasn't one. Nor was there a screen or curtain to pull around me. I lay there starkers, Steve, while she fussed about getting gloves on and preparing the speculum.'

He screwed his face up. 'What's a…what's a speculum?'

'Oh it's a thing to, to…oh it doesn't matter!' I snapped, filling the kettle at the sink. I was badly in need of a cup of tea and couldn't be bothered to explain. 'The weird thing was there was no modesty about the whole experience. I wasn't exactly embarrassed but I did cover my lady bits with my hands while she got ready. It was really quite odd.' I stood gazing out of the kitchen window, thinking about it, while the kettle boiled.

With the tea made, I took the cups and saucers from the dresser, putting them on the table. I turned to Steve and leant back against the countertop, folding my arms.

'Then I went for my mammogram, just across the road. The nurse who showed me into the consulting room was French and…' I stopped talking. Steve was obviously engrossed in something on the laptop. 'Are you listening to me? You asked how I got on so I'm telling you.'

'What? Oh, sorry, yes, go on.' He was contrite, moving his laptop to one side.

'The nurse was French and she didn't speak English. She indicated for me to remove my upper clothing and to leave my things on the chair.' I poured the tea and took a cup over to him. 'I looked around for the gown that's always provided back home but there wasn't one. In Auckland we always wear a gown and when the radiographer's ready, you open one side of it and she manipulates your breast between the plates.' I stopped to draw breath and gulped a welcome mouthful of tea. Steve was still paying attention and listening, probably because I mentioned breasts.

'There I stood, topless, while she put the X-ray plates into the machine. The nurse then manhandled me into the right position, mashing my breast between two icily cold plates. With a quick swivel around and a change of sides, she then flattened the other breast.' I winced, remembering the pain.

'So really, it's much like a hamburger patty, slapped between two buns, wouldn't you say?' Steve smirked and snorted behind his tea cup, enjoying his silly joke. I just rolled my eyes at him and carried on as if I hadn't heard him.

'When the radiographer finished, I reached for my clothing. She said in a very stern voice, "*Non, madame, non, non, non. S'il vous plaît. Arrêter.*" Well I understood that but I thought she meant please stop and wait for your results but she meant stop, don't put your clothes back on. I sat there, Steve, and waited topless for the doctor. I was getting cold and must have waited a full ten minutes with my arms wrapped around my body and covering my breasts. I got the general impression nudity wasn't an issue for French women. They seemed proud of their bodies, no matter what size, which is a great thing. The doctor duly arrived and was very nice.'

I took a sip of tea and continued.

'He was Indian, raised in London and spoke the queen's English. Communication wasn't a problem and he maintained excellent eye contact throughout our conversation. His eyes never moved below my chin as he asked me to lie down and proceeded to squirt gel onto each breast.'

'What a gentleman!' Steve grinned inanely. I ignored that as well.

'During the ultrasound, he completed several circuits with the probe, concentrating hard on the screen in front of him. Throughout the entire procedure, he kept up continuous chit-chat about his life in France, the beauty of New Zealand and how he loved London. I think he was putting me at my ease.'

I finished my tea, putting the cup and saucer in the sink, then collected Steve's from the desk.

'As soon as the specialist finished, he abruptly stood up, declaring there was nothing to worry about, wished me a good day and exited the room.'

'Well that was an experience alright.' Steve slapped his laptop shut and headed for the door. 'I'm off to do some garden work.' He stopped in his tracks and turned. 'Oh and what's for dinner? I'm starving.' That man's stomach ruled his life.

I let out a deep sigh and watched Steve through the window as he traipsed up the steps beside the cottage to the veggie beds. I didn't know why I bothered telling him. All he needed to know was that everything was fine. When he'd asked, 'How did you get on?' I should've just said, 'All good, thanks,' and left it at that. I never learn.

24

Everyday Life

I loved our working day and having friends over for coffee, drinks or dinner when we could and going to their homes to do the same. The balmy summer evenings we spent at Siobhan and Doug's were always outside at the barbecue table, chatting and watching Doug create delicious food on his unconventional and homemade barbecue—the recycled drum of a washing machine. Spicy smoke from his marinated meats and often Steve's favourite sausage—merguez—would waft through the air, making us all salivate. Music played through their large, open, bi-fold kitchen windows where Siobhan passed our salads and drinks to me to ferry to the table. The dogs prowled around Doug's legs, hoping for a little something off the barbecue, while the kids' squeals and happy noise drifted through from the trampoline or the swimming pool.

After dinner when the night came in, I often lay back on the benches wrapped in a blanket with their young son snuggled in tight, watching satellite stations and sometimes shooting stars streak across the deep, star-filled night sky. Out in the country, there's no air pollution and our view was spectacular. It was heaven. These evenings with the family were simple pleasures and all I needed.

One summer evening we went to the tiny hamlet of Aymes, a 45-minute drive from Gaillac, to have dinner with Luke and Catherine, the delightful English/French couple we'd met at the café before the Remembrance service at Castelnau-de-Montmiral.

Their renovated cottage was small but perfectly formed, with two bedrooms and two bathrooms, a kitchen/dining area and a small lounge/living room looking onto a covered terrace and a small garden. Drinks and canapés on the terrace before dinner were compulsory. I vividly remember those lovely evenings, never needing a wrap or sweater.

'Annemarie, do come and see our purchase at the grand sale at Combe de Merigot before your people became the owners.' Catherine's lilting French/English accent was like music to the ear as she led me down the hallway to the spare bedroom. 'Is it not very beautiful?' Catherine proudly introduced me to the large, pale oak armoire standing against the wall. It was a classic French piece with its tapered, black, wrought-iron hinges and latches on the two opening doors.

'It really is, Catherine. I'd be very proud to have that in my home, too.' I ran my hand down the smooth, blonde timber. 'It's beautifully finished.'

Luke arrived in the doorway.

'While you're here, I might as well give you this.' He hauled a wine carton out from inside the armoire. 'I did a stock-up back in the UK and while I was in the wine shop, I picked these up for you.' Luke and Catherine often brought wine back with them as they usually drove across to the UK rather than flying.

Inside the case were six bottles of sauvignon blanc; two were Oyster Bay and four from other New Zealand vineyards I'd never heard of. A lot of estates do change their label for the international market.

'You darling, Luke.' I gave him a big hug. 'What a treat. Thank you so much for getting these. What do I owe you?'

'I've got the receipt somewhere. I'll email it to you with my bank details. No hurry, though.'

We shared one of those bottles with Denise the day she put Harry, her cat, down when he was very ill with an antibiotic-resistant virus. We stood and proposed a solemn toast to dear Harry the Hunter.

Since our arrival in France, Steve hadn't done any proper cycling and now that he'd bought the second-hand bike, he was keen to get out there. Malcolm arrived one Sunday morning to collect him.

'Brace yourself, mate,' Malc warned Steve, slapping him on the shoulder. 'We're doing a three-hour cycle this morning and there are a few hills involved.'

Steve's face was a picture. He was nervous about this ride as it was over a year since he'd done any cycling of that duration, and certainly no hill work.

'C'mon, we'd better get moving. We're meeting Brian and John at the top of the hill. Don't want to keep them waiting, do we?' Malc teased, giving Steve a gentle shove out of the door and winking at me over his shoulder. 'Best you have a hot bath running when you know he's on his way home. He might just be a little sore in the nether regions. *Au revoir*,' he smirked, pulling the door shut behind him.

Steve was most definitely sore when he returned, even after several hot baths, and he sat down very gingerly for the next couple of days.

There was much more to this excursion than just cycling. In New Zealand most of the cycling groups stop for a coffee en route. They do the same in France, too. On this occasion, though, and halfway through the ride, there wasn't only coffee but wine, pastries and other lovely food. I was happy for Steve. It was good for him to have male company, be out cycling and have time away from me. Even if it did result in a very sore bum.

Mary and Symon were enjoying some peace and quiet after a busy weekend with guests before returning to New York. Mary texted me to see if I had an hour free to discuss food for some summer events.

'Morning, Annemarie.' Mary looked up and smiled as I came through the kitchen door with my pen and notebook in hand. 'Help yourself to coffee and come and sit down.' She moved her garden books to one side. 'We're going to have a houseful during the middle weekend in June. There'll be ten of us at this stage,' Mary announced as soon as I settled. 'They're all very relaxed people so I want to keep lunch and dinners fairly casual. Just a couple of courses, with only one course at dinner as there will always be cheese.'

'OK.' I chewed on my pen, thinking. 'Well, if it's going to be casual, how about we do platters for lunch? That's easy. Everyone can then just help themselves. I'll lay it out buffet-style and we'll call it a grazing table. It will still look appetising but informal.'

'Oh, I like the sound of that. Salads, meat platters, breads, cheeses, d'you mean?'

'Exactly that. We can change it each day with different salads and meats. I can also do some sweet things in individual glasses if anyone wants a sugar fix afterwards. Little chocolate mousses, mini lemon tarts, strawberry fools. They're not hard to do and they can go back in the fridge if they're not all eaten, as they'll last a day. What d'you think?'

'That all sounds delicious, Annemarie. Let's do that,' Mary decided. 'Well, that was easy.' She laughed, sitting back in her chair.

'I can make up some dinner menus closer to the time and

email them through to you. I'd like to wait and see what's available at the market around those dates. You can say yea or nay, or add in whatever you would like. Will that work?'

'Perfect! I know Symon will barbecue most evenings so the meat will be taken care of.' Mary was thinking aloud.

'I can do some vegetarian skewers, too, so that'll cover off those that don't eat meat. Maybe Symon could barbecue a whole stuffed fish as well? I could pick one up at the fishmonger's in Gaillac and make a lemon and herb stuffing.'

'Ooh yes, delicious.'

While cooking at Combe de Merigot, I'd started to check first what was in season at the markets and then work a menu around availability. Mary gave me carte blanche with the funds for food but I was always careful and treated her money as I would my own.

'We've plenty of time to finalise everything, Mary. That's one weekend sorted. Anything else?'

We talked on for a bit, discussing household matters. Mary and Symon were expecting a few people coming over the summer, and bedrooms and meals would need to be sorted once we knew firm dates and exact numbers.

They crossed the courtyard that last evening to have a drink and a light supper with us as they were heading back to New York on a very early morning flight out of Toulouse. I would miss them being around; they were so easy to get on with and to work for.

25

A Family Visit

I thought the queen and her entourage had come to stay. The suitcases were huge and there were four of them. My sister Marilyn and her man, Tony, had arrived, and it was just as well I stayed behind when Steve went to collect them from Toulouse train station as there wouldn't have been room for me in the car. To be fair, they'd been travelling in different time and heat zones for a month or more so needed a variety of clothing.

'Hello, dear blister,' I cried with open arms when Mal (as we call her) came through the door. There are six of us girls in my family and a few of us use this silly endearment when we meet up. It was hugs and kisses all round. I'd boiled the kettle many times while going back and forth to the window, waiting for them to swing in the gate and come down the drive. We sat up drinking cups of tea and chatting until 1 a.m. It was exciting finally to have family members visit and introduce them to our beautiful part of France.

Annoyingly the weather was against us the entire time they were with us, not constantly raining but the days were grey. Our first visit was to our wonderful Gaillac market, held every Friday morning. We left Mal and Tony wandering the top square, looking through the clothing, knick-knacks and book stalls, while we hurried down Rue Portal to buy cheese and vegetables in the lower square and at the covered market. Steve and I managed to grab an empty table back at the Conti and scanning the crowd, caught sight of the two of them and waved them over.

'Notice how many older French men stand about gossiping while the wives are doing the shopping, Mal?' I pointed to one particular group while we sat enjoying our coffees.

'Yes, I saw that.' She looked at the men then watched as the women queued up for their fish, meat and vegetables from the market stallholders. 'It's certainly different to how we shop. The men don't usually come with us—ever.'

'Ah, but market day here is such a social occasion for everyone,' I explained. 'It's not just about shopping. It's a time to meet up, exchange family news and generally socialise. You watch; the women will return and there'll be a scramble for tables so groups of them can sit down and talk even longer over their coffee.'

Market-day shopping always took an inordinate amount of time as the stallholders enjoyed a great chat with each customer. Steve took forever at his favourite cheesemaker's van, sampling a little bit of this and a little bit of that, having a chat about texture, taste and smell. Everyone in the queue was so patient. I would've been hopping from one foot to the other and muttering under my breath if I was waiting behind Steve.

'Finished?' I peered into their coffee cups. 'Good. C'mon. We'll walk you around the village so you can get a sense of where and how we live here.' I stood and gathered up our shopping. I loved our town of Gaillac with its picture theatre, many wonderful little boutiques, cafés and restaurants.

Rue Portal was a favourite street of mine. It ran from the top square to the lower one and was home to many gorgeous spots. The kitchen shop, Casseroles et Autres, was a treasure trove and I often went in just to get a fix, admiring all the kitchen gadgetry, tableware and accessories you could ever want. It was owned and run by a super gay couple who always made me feel so welcome, without the pressure to buy. Their little dog slept on his wee bed in a defunct fireplace in the middle of the shop but would rouse himself now and again to trot around, checking out the customers with a little sniff. The owners always beautifully packaged up any purchases, walked you to the door with your parcel and gave you a cheery *au revoir*. The two men went out of their way to source items for you, too.

At the top of Rue Portal sat a little *tabac* run by an older and welcoming Frenchman. He was from Paris so we could always understand him. Well, Steve could. I got snippets of the chat. His *tabac* was a gem of a place, stocking all the English papers, and I'd buy my weekly *Radio Times* from him as we were able to get BBC and ITV programmes in our cottage.

Tantalising and heavenly fragrances of sweet pastry, baked sugary fruit tarts and chocolate enticed us further down Rue Portal and stopped us in our tracks outside Madame Annick Normand's exquisite little *pâtisserie et confiserie* (pastry and confectionery shop). She was such a temptress with her sweets, delightful seasonal fruit tarts, cakes and pretty macarons in every pastel shade, as well as rough slabs of dense chocolate in flavours of milk, dark, white and varying degrees of cocoa solids, all decadently displayed in her front window on cake stands, plates or nestled into metres of ruffled silk.

Going inside was like stepping back in time and into a Parisian café, hidden away in a little side street in, say, the Marais. It was a tiny space but Madame Normand artfully arranged her armchairs and coffee tables, serving tea and coffee in old-fashioned, floral, mismatched cups and saucers—so de rigueur. An old, French wall unit lined the wall behind the marble and glass-fronted cabinet. It also had a glass-fronted cabinet at each end with deep shelves running between the two. These groaned with all manner of delicacies and the famous Monin syrups took up an entire shelf of their own. A wonderful variety of coffees and teas lined another. Steve and I enjoyed morning tea in here several times and I loved the ambience of it all.

Time for lunch and back home I put the kettle on for our cup of tea and set out the gourmet lunch of pickles, baguette, tomatoes, duck pâté, *jambon* (ham), Roquefort and Cantal Vieux cheese Steve had bought from his best friend, the cheesemaker. Steve loves Cantal Vieux, a hard cheese with a strong, earthy smell and flavour. Roquefort has a very pungent odour (some might even go so far as to say it stinks) and is injected with mould, creating the blue veins running through it. It, too, has a strong taste and you can smell it from a hundred paces, no trouble. Both are delicious to me, too. You need to know the kettle is always on when any of my family gets together as we have endless cups of tea, possibly because we talk continuously so we're always thirsty. Not me, though. I don't talk much…

As soon as lunch was done and dusted, we were back in the car, taking Mal and Tony to some of our favourite little villages in the Tarn area. One of these was Villemur-sur-Tarn. Months before, Steve and I had strolled through the maze of the back streets and stopped to enjoy a drink in a bar across from the river. I've investigated the role of the WWII Resistance in the town as so many of the street signs and monuments mention it. To date I haven't found anything, only a reference that the southwest of France was heavily pocketed with cells of partisans and resisters and that they were everywhere through the area.

The decorative brick façade of *la mairie* (the town hall) is particularly attractive. The town clock takes pride of place at the top of the tower and the flowerpots on every windowsill filled with cascading blooms add to its beauty. It sits right on the town square, where anything of any significance takes place. The 13th-century *Tour de Défense* (Defense Tower), right on the river, is a wonderful piece of architecture with its rounded tower and little conical 'top-hat', terracotta-tiled roof.

On we drove along the ridge road to Rabastens, getting

postcard views of sown fields, stands of trees and farmhouses on either side as far as the eye could see.

Mal lounged back in her seat beside me, gazing dreamily out of the car window. 'I just love all the tiny churches and these old farmhouses with their coloured shutters. And look at all the sunflowers and rapeseed. The cities are great for historic places, architecture, galleries and museums but you can't beat the stunning French countryside.' I couldn't agree more and I was glad she could see what I saw and loved about France.

Tony half turned in his front passenger seat to look back at Mal. 'And I can't believe there's no fencing in the fields, Mal.' Tony was a farmer back in New Zealand. 'They use hedging to divide up the paddocks and aren't they immaculate? I love the colours, too.'

The rapeseed was in flower and the fields were a patchwork of yellow and lime.

Marilyn kept us in fits of laughter with her rough pronunciation of the French towns. Her accent was like a physical assault on the ear and hurt each time she tried to say a French word. It became a game while she was with us and I'm sure she deliberately made them sound much worse. She may not have the best ear for languages but is a fantastic cook and baker and makes the most enormous and delicious profiteroles. It's a fight when the family is together to get one on your plate before they disappear. Years ago she explained to us younger sisters how you make them, pronouncing the choux pastry 'chucks'. It took us a few minutes to register what she meant. It was hilarious at the time and the rest of us siblings have never let her forget it. You can imagine her interpretation, then, of the French street signs—diabolical!

Saturday morning I whizzed Mal and Tony up to Puycelsi, classed as one of the most beautiful villages in France, a status the tourism board have given to many villages in France. They both loved this fortified town, even though we were sightseeing with umbrellas up and zipped into thick jackets. Mal had to make do with postcards to compensate for the lack of decent photos. All too soon it was time to hit the road to get to Doug and Siobhan's for a coffee. They'd come for dinner the night before and invited Mal and Tony to stop in and see their little piece of heaven in the countryside.

We spent our afternoon in Albi exploring Sainte-Cécile d'Albi Cathedral, the beautiful boutiques and pretty back streets. The audio guide in the cathedral took us all off to various points to listen and learn. The treasury holds 15th-century chalices, ordination robes and exquisite gold crosses. It's incredible to see such pieces and to try and comprehend their antiquity. Albi Cathedral was built in 1282 and is the largest brick structure in the world. The most extensive collection of Italian Renaissance frescoes in France covers the entirety of the vaulted ceiling. These 16th-century mural paintings are pastoral and biblical scenes, set against an azure-blue background, and they catch your eye and take your breath away as soon as you walk in. It's so impressive, belying the fact the church there has a bloody history of crusades against the Cathars, also known as Albigensians as they first established themselves in Albi. The cathedral is the focal point of tourism for Albi.

'You boys can look after yourselves while Mal and I have a look around the shops and find some flowers to take to CH. We'll meet you at the usual café on the square, Steve. You know the one. See you in an hour,' I called over my shoulder.

CH had invited us all for drinks and to see her little château and garden.

'Keep your purse in your handbag, Mal.' Tony winked at her as she loved to shop. She didn't even acknowledge that she'd heard him, just slipped her arm through mine and held her head high as we walked away.

CH poured champagne and offered foie gras canapés along with a smoked fish pâté and local dried meats when we sat down in her little salon off the kitchen. Pierre was home and joined us for drinks and a chat about his books and busy life writing. I could hear Mal oohing and aahing as CH toured Tony and her around the home and garden. It's a beautiful place and each room has been lovingly restored and dressed in exquisite fabrics and furniture restored or modernised by CH's own hand.

On each level the round tower and turret side of the château had been renovated into an en-suite for the bedroom next to it. CH was very talented and did lots of the work herself and made up her own colours and daubs for the old stone floors and walls. She'd renovated one of the crumbling stone buildings in her garden, creating the most elegant dining room. Two ornate chandeliers hung over the large dining table and CH had placed large, carved and gilt armchairs and coffee tables in the two back corners. Heavy, lustrous gold drapes hung from enormous brass rails and were held back with large and ornate Venetian ceramic and silk tassels either side of the French doors which opened out into her garden. This was her summer entertaining room.

Several hours on it was time for us to leave. We'd had a busy day and there was still a long drive back to our place. Everyone was stifling yawns and I'd yet to make dinner for us all.

'Thank you so very much, CH,' I said, kissing her goodbye. 'You've been most kind having us here at your home. It's been lovely.'

'Yes, CH, thank you very much for your hospitality.' It was Mal's turn to say goodbye. 'It's been such a treat to come to a château and home like yours.'

'Not at all, Marilyn.' CH smiled graciously. 'So very nice to meet you and Tony. Enjoy the rest of your stay. Annemarie, I'll see you in a couple of days at Merigot. I have some curtains to hang.'

Our next trip out was to the market in the medieval town of St-Antonin-Noble-Val. This town is every tourist's dream and where Tony bought a smart black French beret at the wonderful Sunday market.

'How d'you like this, Mal?' He turned the beret to a jaunty angle on his head. 'I think I'll wear it when I'm working around the farm,' he teased.

'You will not! It's far too good for that,' Mal scolded him.

Tony also treated himself to a Panama hat, which he promptly donned and wore all day. It was a good thing as he was easy to spot in the market crowd when we all got separated.

Mal was having a lovely time, wandering from stall to stall, shop to shop, buying gifts and souvenirs for the family at home. I stowed baguettes, cheese, heavenly vine-ripened tomatoes, aged cheese and cooked sausage in my basket for our picnic lunch. The sausage was too hard to resist and the cooking aromas always drew people deeper into the market, as did the three musicians set up under the plane tree beside the café in the little square. The market was humming and it was cheek by jowl at every stall. It's such a popular place and made even more popular by the movie *The Hundred-Foot Journey* as it was filmed in and around St-Antonin-Noble-Val.

We meandered slowly back to the car and laid out our lunch on one of the picnic tables beside the river. Steve pulled out the knife and plastic bread board we kept in the car for impromptu lunches and sliced everything up. Once we'd eaten and brushed off the breadcrumbs, we hopped back in the car and were off again to visit the hilltop town of Cordes-sur-Ciel. We zigzagged our way up the steep, cobbled streets to the parapet to show Mal and Tony the outstanding views over dense, forested valleys. It started to drizzle so the boys ducked into a bar for a beer while Mal and I carried on, exploring the little boutiques and making our way gingerly down the wet and now slippery cobbles to the car park to wait for them.

Time for another cup of tea and a lie down (as the saying goes in our family) so it was good to get back in the car and trundle home. Steve went off to do errands while I made a start on dinner and Mal sat and chatted with me in the kitchen and wrote her postcards home. Tony whistled up Indy and the two of them went out for a companionable walk around the vineyard while there was a dry spell.

It was an early rise for a quick breakfast and a speedy departure. Mal and Tony had packed their bags after last night's dinner and their luggage sat waiting at the front door. No prolonged farewells; just kisses and hugs. Steve was dropping them back to Toulouse station from where they would continue their European holiday. I stood waving till the car disappeared through the gates at the top of the drive. Tilly and Indy dashed in ahead of me as I turned into the cottage and closed the door behind us. It was time to do dishes, strip beds, clean the bathroom and get the laundry on. Keeping busy left me little time to dwell on when I would see any of my family again.

Steve rushed in the door after dropping Mal and Tony off and disappeared into the downstairs bathroom. I thought he must have been busting to go. He came into the kitchen grinning.

'What's making you grin like an idiot?' His grin was infectious and I couldn't help but smile myself.

He started laughing and could hardly get the words out.

'When they were here, I kept moving the dog shampoo to the shelf under the basin but each day I found it back on the edge of the bath. I've just realised why. The label's in French so Tony didn't realise what it was, did he?' More silly laughter. 'He was using the dog shampoo all the time they were here.' Steve was snorting by now and I couldn't help but laugh out loud as well. 'We should have checked to see whether…to see whether he had a nice glossy coat before he left.' Steve had to sit down then, roaring at his silly joke.

We never did tell Mal and Tony.

26

News Flash

After a nerve-racking five weeks during which Steve couldn't breathe a word, he accepted a job in New Zealand after an old work colleague had contacted him and he'd undergone a Skype interview. You'll be shocked, I know. *We* were shocked as the opportunity was totally out of the blue.

We'd talked about it endlessly, going over the pros and cons during those five weeks, having plenty of time to mull everything over.

'What d'you think?' Steve turned in his seat to look at me the night he got the offer. 'I'm not likely to get another chance like this in a hurry and I don't want to spend too many more years mowing lawns. Later when I've retired, yes, but not now. I do love it here but right now I'd like to use my brain again.'

'I get it. I really do.' I was leaning against the kitchen doorframe, thinking. 'We do have to consider our financial future, too. Then there's Callum to think about, as well as Margot.'

Steve's sister was responding well to treatment. This was another reason to return so there would be quality time with her.

'My worry is Mary and Symon.' My stomach flipped over

every time I said their names. 'When they took us on, we said we'd be here a couple of years. I feel like we've deceived them and they'll think badly of us. They've got so much going on here over the summer and I don't want to be letting them down; they've been so very good to us, Steve.' When I thought about telling them, I felt sick.

'I know. The thing is I didn't go looking for a job. It came looking for me. But yes, that will be the hard bit, telling them,' he admitted.

'I've been thinking and I've got a suggestion to make.' I wasn't quite sure how to frame the words. 'How would you feel if I stayed on for the summer?' I hurried on before he could speak. 'We could ask Malc to step in for you with the garden work. He could also do the airport runs when I can't. Sort the car, the pool, etc.,' I said, watching Steve's reaction. 'That way, there are no worries for Mary and Symon in terms of housekeeping and cooking for them and their summer guests, and the grounds and cars would be well looked after. Everything would continue smoothly and it would give them plenty of time to find our replacements.'

Steve didn't answer for a minute. 'I'm not sure,' he murmured eventually. I could see his brain working. 'We're supposed to be going with Andy and Emma to their Dorset home in late August and then there's our trip to Puglia with the Auckland gang in September.'

'It's late. Let's sleep on it. We can talk more in the morning,' I said firmly. 'I'm just taking the girls out for a last wee.' I bent to lace up my shoes and went out into the garden, pondering on it all myself while the dogs snuffled around, finding just the right spot. How would I be on my own for three months? Was it fair to Steve, too, leaving him to return to New Zealand alone?

'Be quick,' I said to Tilly and Indy. 'It's a bit chilly out here, girls. C'mon.' Tilly hated having to go out at night and took so long to get on with it when she got there. Their business finally done, they rushed past me and into their beds in the laundry.

'It's time for bed, Steve,' I said, coming back into the living room. 'You coming up?'

'I'll be there shortly. I just want to have a think.' He turned back to his laptop.

At breakfast the following morning, I raised the dilemma again.

'I was thinking if you *did* go back on your own, you could return to London for the last week in August. I'll have a couple of nights with Andy and Emma in Dulwich Village then the three of us could collect you from Heathrow and drive straight down to Dorset. That might work.' I concentrated on buttering my toast and Steve continued munching through his cereal, listening to me. 'Then once we're back in London, we can fly to Puglia to meet up with the others. We'll be apart for, what, 12 to 15 weeks? We can do it. It actually works perfectly if you return to New Zealand in May as the rental contract is up on our house then. You could stay a couple of nights with one of our friends then move back into our place.'

Steve stood up, put his empty bowl in the sink and dropped his bread in the toaster. He leant up against the counter, facing me, with folded arms.

'You seem to have it all worked out,' he said. 'And it all sounds feasible. OK, if you're happy to stay, I'll return and start the job. It seems to be the right thing to do for Mary and Symon. The time will pass quickly with me learning the ropes. I can stay late at work if needs be and not think about you having dinner ready at home.'

Taking out the financial future factor, it was a tough decision to make. France had inveigled her way under our skin and had become part of who we now were. The places we'd seen, the experiences we'd had and the people we'd met were firmly embedded in our consciousness. The predominant memories would be the people who'd come into our lives and working for Mary and Symon at Combe de Merigot.

I didn't want to call Mary and Symon out of the blue to tell them Steve would be returning to New Zealand so we sent an email explaining and offering for me to stay on for the summer, outlining how the property, and they, would be looked after. This would give them time to digest the news before we talked by phone. I was so nervous.

Luckily for us, after their initial shock, they were understanding and supportive. Both were very happy for me to stay on and work with them over the summer, with Malc coming in to look after the grounds and do airport runs when I couldn't, as well as all the other bits and pieces Steve took care of.

There was a flurry of activity, booking airline tickets and sorting out how I would progress alone. Life was going to be very different. I hadn't been on my own or lived by myself for nearly 30 years. It would be a completely new experience but an opportunity to see how I would cope. I was scared and excited, all at the same time.

We booked Steve's imminent departure and his subsequent return to London at the end of August. After our Dorset stay with Andy and Emma, we'd fly with Ginny and Dave from London to Naples for a few days, hire a car and explore Pompeii and Herculaneum then drive on to Puglia together. Our Auckland friend Kevin had found an enormous, elegant villa there for our group of ten. It would be a fun week of wine, food and friendship as well as an opportunity to explore a fabulous, unspoilt area on the southeastern tip of Italy.

Malc and Ruth put on a last, beautiful lunch before Steve left, inviting our friends and theirs. Both were excellent cooks and just asked the rest of us to bring wine; they would deal with the food. Ruth had soaked raw beetroot in olive oil and balsamic vinegar overnight, adding crumbled goat's cheese, toasted walnuts and caper berries just before serving. Out came the main of roasted cod loin with an olive and sun-dried tomato tapenade, confit potatoes as well as a platter of steamed green beans. All so delicious. Ruth's finale was her classic tarte au citron. What a lunch. I have no idea what time we got home but it was well past 10 p.m. Can you see I'm giving you the French (Gallic) shrug? This indicates that that was just what happened when we went to Ruth and Malc's for lunch, and we could do nothing about it. Not that we wanted to!

My finish time at Combe de Merigot was mid-August. I would stay a couple of nights with Siobhan and Doug and then fly to London, catching a bus from the airport to stay with my cousin Catherine in Banbury to have a few days exploring the Cotswolds with her. Catherine was hoping to come to Gaillac for a couple of days before I finished with Mary and Symon but I wasn't making any further plans just then. My focus was on helping Steve get ready to return to New Zealand and Mary and Symon's first big event with the family and ten guests. After that, I would be able to think straight again and plan a little more.

Mary and Symon, too, were making adjustments, deciding how they were going to run things when I finished, eventually deciding not to replace us. It was a busy time of discussions and planning. Tilly and Indy would return to London as there would no longer be guardians living at Combe de Merigot. Separate friends of ours would take over the running of the place, one doing the garden and the other looking after the house, both living offsite.

In the meantime there was plenty for us to do. Steve's working life revolved around the weather forecast. He was tackling the spring growth, trying to complete jobs held up with the rain and liaising with our French tradespeople, two being garden specialists from Lombard Nature garden centre in Lisle-sur-Tarn. Some of the yew trees in the semi-circular hedge were dead and needed replacing. These two came in and replaced them and planted an avenue of cypress trees and a stand of some 30 poplar trees to soften a fairly rough paddock. Steve worked with them to get it all done, enjoying the male camaraderie. They also planted a bank of heavenly, fragrant and deep-purple lavender at the base of the horseshoe yew hedge. It looked and smelt divine and I loved to trail my hand through it to release its intoxicating perfume.

27

A Change in Direction

Steve's departure date was getting closer and closer. An overnight visit to the Millau Viaduct, the village of Conques and to the Roquefort caves where the cheese 'grows' was on our to-do list as well as planning Steve's farewell dinner party. We'd invited about 25 people, a mix of French and English. All the English people coming spoke French so our French friends would be comfortable mixing and chatting. Steve and I had bought a good-sized paella pan and burner in a closing-down sale so I planned a chorizo, chicken and prawn paella with bowls of green salads, platters of asparagus, roasted tomatoes and various breads. I was trying to make it a stress-free and easy evening. Dessert was simple—mini vanilla ice creams, chocolate brownie squares and mini lemon tarts. The ice creams came from a fabulous frozen foods store called Picard in Gaillac. I was excited to discover frozen legs of New Zealand lamb in there, too.

The summer dining room at the poolside was the perfect place to have drinks and dinner. There was an enormous fireplace so we could have a roaring fire all night. Symon had a great sound system in place which we could plug iPods and laptops into. We hoped to be dancing until the wee hours, with no one actually falling into the pool.

It was even more important now, knowing we were leaving, to absorb everything and to commit our experiences to memory. On one of Steve's last weekends, we drove the back country roads to Brian and Suzanna's for dinner. Ruth and Malc had introduced us some months earlier, and the four of them had come to dinner at ours. What a night! Suzanna came through our door talking so I knew I'd most definitely met my kindred spirit. Don't ask me what I made for dinner but afterwards the dishes were stacked high in the kitchen sink, the coffee table and chairs pushed up against the wall, the carpet rolled up and we danced and sang until the wee hours. I have no idea what time I chivvied them out of the door but the stack of bottles in the laundry the next morning would probably have told a story all of its own. And guess what? I lost my voice. I must've picked up a bug or something…certainly couldn't have been all the talking and singing.

Anyway, we were now on our way to spend the evening at theirs. The wheat fields swayed and danced in the light evening breeze and the creamy stone of the old farmhouses and *pigeonnier* stood illuminated in the evening sun which was casting the most glorious, shimmering golden light.

'Look and remember, Steve.' My eyes were feasting on the disappearing view as we drove. 'This beautiful countryside, the history of the places we've seen and the people who've come into our lives. We've had such wonderful times and laughed so much.' I stopped for a moment. 'I'm just thankful we've been given this time to share and enjoy it all. How privileged and lucky are we?' My eyes were starting to fill at the thought of leaving.

'I know, I know,' he muttered. His eyes were on the road ahead but I knew he wasn't seeing anything. His mind was elsewhere.

Suzanna and Brian were in the middle of renovating their old farmhouse and had cleared out a small stone barn ready to host us, Malc and Ruth and another couple. The barn still housed an ancient bread oven and old rabbit hutches, once home to rabbits that used to be raised for the kitchen table. Not a bunny in sight the night we were there. Suzanna had cleaned the hutches out and filled them with candles and decorative items. The barn resembled someone's country dining room and was so cosy, with a fire roaring in the old bread oven. She'd laid an inviting dining table with a multi-coloured table cloth, cutlery and glassware, candles and flowers. They'd strung fairy lights around the interior walls and these, combined with the fire's glow and candles, created such a wonderful ambience.

Suzanna and Brian were brilliant cooks. Dinner was a delicious lemon risotto topped with scallops and a sprinkling of lemon zest, followed by a main of pork belly, garlic mash and local cabbage. They plated up exquisite vanilla meringues and a tiny chocolate mousse for our dessert.

We followed it soon after with another memorable dinner with our French neighbours, Olivier and Clotilde, along with Ann and Bruno. We'd been looking forward to it as Olivier had been preparing *cassoulet* (a slow-cooked casserole of several meats and white beans) for two days. It reduced down to the most delicious, unctuous texture and taste. My contribution was dessert. I had a minor panic when we arrived as dinner wasn't just for the six of us; it was for all six children as well. The French are all about family, which I do love, and I should have thought about that before making dessert. We managed. It was a little like the dividing of the loaves and fishes but everyone had plenty to eat. The *cassoulet* melted in our mouths and was so divine I went back for a second helping.

An English friend once commented on how well behaved French children were, both in restaurants and at their own table. He put it down to the children always sitting down with the adults for every meal, from the time they could sit in a chair. That made sense as we never saw children running wild around a restaurant or the family table. Our experience at Olivier and Clotilde's and at Ann and Bruno's had been that the children were also helpful. They would clear plates and help serve food. Along with their parents, they welcomed us at the door, raising their faces for the two-cheek kiss. They were so sweet and very polite. We were well and truly in the habit of the two-cheek kiss every time we met friends, be it in the street, when they arrived at our home or us at theirs. It was such a welcoming gesture.

I really admire many French country ways and one is how Sunday is dedicated to family. People we met thought nothing of driving one and a half hours to have a long lunch with other family members—siblings, parents, grandparents, everyone was involved. Our experience was that the big supermarkets—Le Clerc, Carrefour and Aldi—were closed on Sunday but you could still pick up everything you wanted from a Sunday market or a 8 à Huit store that had reduced Sunday hours. *Boulangeries*, however, could trade any day of the year as bread is the staff of life. The two-hour lunch was followed almost religiously by tradespeople and some shops did this, too, but most wanted to catch the lunchtime trade so remained open or just closed for a one-hour lunch break.

Yes, it did take some adjustment but how sensible were the French? Closed shops meant more time with family. Time to eat at the table with family. I was all for it.

28

Home Alone

The day of Steve's farewell party was a miserable, wet and windy one. I kept glancing up at the skies while we were setting up the summer dining room, praying for sunshine and for the wind to die down. It didn't happen. I emailed everyone to suggest they dress warmly as we would be semi-outdoors. There just wouldn't have been room for us all in our kitchen-cum-diner-cum-lounge.

Not to worry, the fire was roaring and it helped a lot. Malcolm set himself up to one side, nurturing the paella along for me, and Steve was on the gate, welcoming our guests and pouring the drinks as they arrived. It took forever to say hello with all those kisses being exchanged as well as an excited *bonsoir*. Everyone lined up with their plates and Malcolm heaped steaming mounds of delicious paella onto them as the guests filed past before finding a place at the table and helping themselves to salads and bread. After dessert Steve made a touching speech in French. With a catch in his voice, he thanked all those who'd welcomed us into their homes, their lives and their country. I was wiping my eyes and my nose constantly. It must have been colder than I thought...

A cheer went up and Steve received a great round of

applause. Everyone hugged and kissed him and wished him well. I turned the music up; we pushed the chairs back and the night continued. We finished up around 1 a.m. after a fun and poignant evening, and luckily no one fell in the pool.

After being together constantly for such a long time, life would be very different without Steve around. We met up in the garden for morning coffee, to eat lunch together then to have a late-afternoon cup of tea on the garden bench outside the atelier. I wasn't sure how I felt about being alone.

It hadn't been easy at times, for either of us. We'd never worked together before and both of us have strong characters and ways of doing things. Some days you could've cut the air with a knife. Thank heavens we were in the countryside, with no near neighbours to hear our raised voices. Other days it was a joy to be together and on our own on such a stunning estate. We'd learnt so much about how the other operated.

It was time to move into separate phases of our working lives again and we agreed it was a good thing. Steve would enjoy peace and quiet at home, too, but *only* for the first week. Well, that's what I was telling him as I was sure he'd miss my chatter after that. Of course Tilly and Indy would enjoy listening to my 10,000 words a day… Truth be told, they would probably slink off to their basket in the laundry and put their paws over their ears.

Luckily I'd made a few friends and wouldn't be on my own all the time.

The next day, Château de Saurs, on a back road to Lisle-sur-Tarn, was having an open garden and cellar day. Both of us had wanted to visit since we'd arrived and Steve had added it to his must-do list. The owner was Monsieur Yves Burrus and as we wandered the garden, who should be out there with his dog but Monsieur Burrus himself. It wasn't possible to walk past him without an acknowledgement. Steve shook his hand and we both said *bonjour*. Another couple arrived behind us.

'I hope you're enjoying the garden?' Monsieur Burrus politely inquired. 'Would you like to see where we store the wine?'

The four of us promptly chorused, 'Yes, thank you,' and he turned and guided us down old, mossy stone steps and into his magnificent, cool cellar. With its ancient, brick-vaulted ceiling arching above us, the architecture of the enormous room was beautiful. Rows and rows of wine barrels ran for about a kilometre under the château itself. As with most winemakers in the area, they made a variety of reds and whites.

At the cellar door, we stopped to sample rosé and one of the reds. Siobhan and Doug had booked us to have a last dinner with them and Doug Senior so we bought a special bottle of red to take with us.

On the Monday morning, Steve threw back the bed covers, leapt out of bed and marched off to the bathroom.

'I'm not leaving France without seeing the Millau Viaduct or the Roquefort caves. D'you think the dog sitter would be able to have Tilly and Indy for the night if we went this morning?'

'Hang on, we're supposed to be at Malc and Ruth's for coffee today.' I was still rubbing the sleep from my eyes and fumbled for my phone. 'I have no idea if the dog sitter's even in town, Steve. You'll just have to hold your horses while I find out.' I quickly found the number, hoping 7:30 a.m. wasn't too early to send a text. *Better than ringing*, I thought. My phone pinged back a couple of minutes later.

'You're very lucky,' I shouted over the noise of the shower. 'We can drop the dogs off any time.'

'Excellent,' came the muffled response.

I punched in an apology message to Malc and Ruth, asking for their forgiveness and explaining Steve's great rush, and grabbed two overnight bags from the wardrobe, threw some toiletries and my clothes in one, having no idea what the weather would be like. It was a quick dash through the shower for me followed by an even quicker breakfast.

Poor Tilly and Indy were a little bewildered with all the rushing around. I threw their beds, food and them in the back seat, making sure I had their leads and Tilly's meds with me. We made a brief stop at the dog sitter to drop them off and then we were on the road again.

Our first stop was the outstanding medieval village of Conques, hidden in the Aveyron valley. Without the signposts, you would never know it was there as it's so well hidden. The Sainte-Foy Abbey in the centre was a popular stop for pilgrims in the 800s on their journey to Santiago de Compostela, Spain. Many such stops and routes exist throughout this area and other parts of Europe, all leading to this religious destination. The original monastery at Conques was 8th century and built by monks fleeing the Saracens. The village is a beautiful and ancient one with many stories attached to it.

We had every intention of staying the night and even booked a room but over lunch we decided there was too much to see and do elsewhere and cancelled our reservation. The exuberant restaurant owner stood in the doorway, jabbering at full speed and gesticulating left and right, giving us directions for the picturesque route, through the villages of Estaing and Espalion. It was an easy, meandering road through sun-dappled forests, opening out to views of the River Lot now and then.

How I would have loved to explore Estaing but all I could do was crane my neck to take in the disappearing view of a sweet little village as we whizzed over the Gothic bridge. It straddles the Lot and is crossed by hundreds of pilgrims each year on their way to Santiago de Compostela. I only managed a glimpse of the vast, wrought-iron cross, a symbol of the Aveyron region, when we coasted over the water. Steve was on a mission—only one stop permitted!

I managed to convince him to pull over and to stretch our legs at Espalion, however, and drink our coffee right beside the old stone bridge and river. Espalion has some beautiful old tannery buildings still standing on the right bank and dating from when the leather trade was a major industry in the town. Each tannery is equipped with a wide stone ledge for washing the hides. Another feature of Espalion is the Old Palace which has several beautiful round towers and turrets and is built in a lovely old brick. We just didn't have enough time to explore properly. On we drove to the home of the famous French knives —Laguiole.

The weather turned miserable and cold. I longed for my winter clothing and thick jacket which were hanging in the wardrobe back at Merigot. All I had was a thin jacket and ballet flats to wear. Steve was even less equipped and had only packed a sweatshirt as we'd left home in such a hurry.

Regardless of the weather, we explored Laguiole. I've always admired the colourful, elegant lines and weight of Laguiole cutlery and was very keen to get a set of knives. I knew they would be the real thing here, with the proper little bee insignia at the base of the handle. Many fakes are produced worldwide so you need to be careful what and where you buy the cutlery. The price is usually a giveaway. However, I changed my mind once I saw these prices, ranging from €100 upwards for just four knives. I decided I didn't need or love them enough to splash out.

Our bed for the night was at an *auberge* right in the middle of town which also offered dinner and breakfast. It was nothing fancy but perfectly comfortable and clean. Steve had to have the famous *aligot* with his dinner. *Aligot* is creamed potatoes, made very elastic with the addition of a stretchy Cantal or tomme cheese and laden with heavy cream, butter and salt. The waiter inquired if I was on a diet as I'd politely declined when he asked whether *madame* would also be having *aligot*. He visibly slumped before me and was so crestfallen that I said, 'Oh, go on then. I'll have a little.' He lit up like a light, beaming at me. It was pretty tasteless to me and I could only assume the fuss must be all about the texture.

Next morning, at a very chilly 4°C, we trundled along the high road through to Marvejols. The temperature plummeted even further as we drove. At one stage it was only 1°C and snow was lying in the ditches. The countryside was rugged and beautiful—undulating green hills, stone cottages, crafted stone walls, and some very shaggy cattle that mimicked the Highland coo. It was like a Scottish landscape too, and so very different from the Tarn region.

Coming on this little sojourn with us was a bidet, wrapped in heavy blankets in the boot. Yes, a bidet. Why are you surprised? I'm married to Steve, after all… Mary wanted to get rid of surplus materials from the renovations at Merigot and to clear space in the garage. So Steve had listed the items on Le Bon Coin's website, similar to eBay, Etsy or Trade Me in New Zealand. A lady in Marvejols had bought the bidet and Steve decided that as the town was only a little off the beaten track, we would take it with us and deliver it on our way to the Millau Viaduct. Once we found the lady, we parked the cars side by side and Steve transferred the bidet from one boot to the other. *Madame* explained to Steve her bedroom was on the top floor of her house but the bathroom was on the ground floor. This bidet would be plumbed in somewhere near her bedroom, saving *madame* a long trek in the night when she got the call of nature. Too much information, some would say, between total strangers…

Marvejols is a welcoming and pretty town and, as is typical of France, has a fascinating history of being sacked and rebuilt. Its three beautiful, fortified gates from the 17th century—the Soubeyran, Théron and Chanelles—as well as its pedestrian shopping streets, make it a lovely place to wander, explore and shop.

With the boot lid slammed shut, it was time for us to head for Millau. We had no intention of crossing the viaduct; we wanted to go under it to get a sense of the sheer size of the impressive steel and concrete structure. The transporter trucks crossing it looked like Tonka toys. It's the tallest viaduct in the world and connects Paris to Barcelona. Designed by an Englishman, Sir Norman Foster, the cost to build it was an eye-popping €320 million. It's a sight to be seen.

Our tour of the Roquefort caves was excellent although a little drawn-out for maximum impact before we could even get to see the cheese. The cellars, with seeping, mildewy walls and ceilings, were very wet underfoot. I don't know how deep we went but it was down quite a few flights of stairs and it got colder and colder as we descended. Some of these caves can be 300 metres deep. It was disappointing not to see people working and injecting the cheese with penicillin but I thought they could easily scrape it off some of the walls we walked past, they were so green with mould. We did eventually get to see the whole process via a video.

Despite the cooler weather and heavy skies, our few days driving the circuit of the interior of the Massif Central were fantastic. The countryside was glorious and some of the towns were picture-postcard material. France is just so beautiful and I would strongly recommend skimming major tourist attractions and focusing on lesser places such as Estaing, Espalion, Marvejols and Laguiole. You absorb the true essence of France this way, enjoying the lunchtime three-course *plat du jour* in a hidden village and avoiding the 'tat' and push-and-shove of the bigger and more well-known places.

We didn't have time on this last-minute trip but usually we Googled the villages and tourist offices for any events that were happening and tried to get to places early in the day to beat the crowds and the heat. We could always have a little lie down and a snooze in the afternoon after our wine and *plat du jour*.

There are so many feast, harvest and other traditional days celebrated with street processions and bands in France. Everyone joins in and the events are so much fun. During July and August, some villages have these very convivial communal dinners once a week. The villagers string bunting up around the square, creating a carnival atmosphere, and trucks arrive late morning to offload all the trestle tables and chairs. Everyone pitches in to help arrange them so as many people as possible can fit in. The food trucks arrive late afternoon and it's not long before delicious aromas start wafting through open windows and doors, drawing the villagers out into the square for dinner. Speakers are set up at strategic points; the music begins and everyone finds a place to sit, pull out the wine, beer and glasses and cutlery and crockery before they do the rounds of the trucks, choosing what they would like for dinner. The dinners aren't just for the villagers; people arrive from all around the area as well as those on tour. They're entertaining French evenings and not to be missed.

Back home, Denise, Malcolm and Ruth came in to say goodbye to Steve. All these goodbyes were making me teary. Two nights before Steve left, we took Doug and Siobhan out for dinner. It was a small way of saying thank you for everything they'd done for us—opening their home to us when we'd lost ours after we were thrown out of Mas de Lavande and then helping us secure our rewarding job with Mary and Symon. After our dinner out and a nightcap at ours, it was time for Siobhan and Doug to say their goodbyes, too. Siobhan shed a few tears which set me off again. They'd been exceptional friends and I knew Steve would very much miss spending time with them.

I cried at the airport the next day as Steve and I said goodbye for three months. You already know it wasn't easy at times, working together. This aside, it had been the most special time for the two of us and I now felt so flat and tearful. When I got back from the airport, I took myself out to sit on the bench seat in the garden, sipping a cup of tea in between sobs. Indy leapt up to sit beside me, pushing her body against mine and placing a paw on my lap. Sweet girl. She was trying to comfort me and I pulled her in close. Dogs just know when you're upset.

Twenty-four hours on and with a good sleep under my belt, I felt more like my old self and got on with what needed doing. The day dawned a stunning one, albeit a little chilly. The sky was azure blue and cradling a blazing sun.

'Come on, girls,' I called, lifting their leads off the hook in the laundry room. Both dogs arrived at full tilt, skidding on the floor tiles. 'No need to call you twice then.' I laughed, bending down to rub their heads. It was difficult to lever the door open as they were so excited, scrabbling to get out for their walk. They always went a little crazy for the first few minutes outside so I left them to rush about and just stood breathing deeply and taking in the beautiful day and the peace and quiet. If I was seriously religious, I would have blessed myself. How privileged was I to live in such a stunning and serene part of the world?

Home again and with the dogs snoozing happily in their beds, I put the kettle on for coffee. Coffee for one. I'd get used to it. No point in dwelling on being alone. It was time to get moving.

First job was to dead-head the roses at the front of the house and then start setting up for summer. I whisked the dust sheets off the outdoor chairs in the atelier and pulled out the hurricane lamps and wall decorations. With my music on in the summer dining room, I spent the afternoon dancing back and forth to the atelier, collecting all the bits and pieces, lining up the rattan chairs and coffee table, hanging wall ornaments and banging the sofa cushions into shape. I filled the fireplace with dry logs to complete the picture. What a relaxing haven it would be to sit and eat beside the pool in the coming months or just to sit and read in the outdoor chairs in the shade.

Denise was coming to help fill my first real evening alone. We'd share my dinner of duck breast, lentils, asparagus and a salad. A bottle of local Gaillac wine was chilling in the fridge and I was looking forward to her company and an enjoyable end to a glorious day.

29

A Good Weekend

The late-afternoon sun streamed languidly through the open French doors, warming the burnished terracotta tiles. A soft breeze and the thrum of the tractor weaving in and out of the vineyard rows filtered through. Dust motes swirled in the sun's rays, and out on the terrace, bees, heavy with pollen, buzzed drunkenly from one lavender pot to the next. It was a soporific and drowsy afternoon after a rather hectic long weekend looking after Mary, Symon and many of their friends.

One guest arrived with a dozen bottles of Ruinart Champagne plus a dozen bottles of what looked to be vintage French red wine. Another brought a huge foie gras which was sliced and passed around with blinis. Someone else had caught a salmon in an Alaskan river, had it smoked and sent on ice to himself in London then he brought it as a gift to say thank you to Mary and Symon for their hospitality. What fabulous house guests! The wine flowed with plenty of food throughout the days and all the guests entered into the spirit of the weekend.

They began arriving on the Friday morning and I was on duty for a casual lunch for eight in the summer dining room. They sat down to *pissaladière* (caramelised onion, anchovy and black olive tarts), sweet cherry tomato and pesto tarts, a mixed green salad with a balsamic dressing and a red and white endive salad with a Dijon mustard dressing plus breads. No dessert, but a delicious selection of French cheeses followed. On Friday evening the chef, Jean-Luc, came in to cook. Mary had engaged him the summer before and enjoyed his food. He'd prepared dinner to Mary's specifications—simple—and so it was.

Jean-Luc did all the prep offsite so it was straightforward for him to finish off and assemble at the house. He and I shook hands in the car park and together we carried everything upstairs into the kitchen. My contribution for the evening was canapés—small bites of local duck pâté on crispy baguette rounds and smoked salmon, dill and crème fraîche with a few drops of tabasco on cucumber rounds. These disappeared very quickly while the guests were mingling and having an *apéro* in the balmy evening sun on the back terrace, amongst the potted lavenders and with a stunning vista of vines and forest.

Mary and I had dressed the table in the summer dining room, keeping it informal but elegant with the crystal glasses, napkins and candles, interlaced with little terracotta lavender pots and trails of ivy. Classical music played softly through the sound system.

Jean-Luc produced a dressed quinoa and bulgur wheat salad as a starter that contained little bites of colourful, blanched vegetables and nuts. He'd made radish flowers which he placed strategically on the top. Alongside he laid a fan of mangetouts. The main course was three small, skewered veal rounds accompanied by a red-wine jus and crispy, baked potato croquettes. The cheese course was the lightest, mousse-like goat's cheese I'd ever tasted or seen. It was so silky, softly tangy and slid over the tongue. He laid this on a small plate, accompanied by a prune coulis he'd made. The two flavours together were so complementary and divine. Macerated strawberries with fresh strawberries on the side, along with a pretty tuile basket he'd created and filled with tuile biscuits, were his grand finale.

Jean-Luc was a very relaxed and mild-mannered chef and we had fun together. His English was limited, so was my French, but we got along famously. He and I tripped up and down the side staircase with each course and out to the summer dining room with plates stacked up our arms. We ate our mini-meals together of whatever was left over from each course, perched on a chair at the kitchen table, with Jean-Luc asking me after each little bite, 'You like?'

'Oh yes, Jean-Luc. I like very much,' I replied, licking my lips.

After we'd cleared the main away, Symon must have felt it was safe to pour us each a glass of exquisite, velvety-smooth red wine. Jean-Luc, who never left the area, asked in all innocence whether it was a local Gaillac wine. Well, I spluttered through my mouthful at that comment. These people were drinking stunning Bordeaux and Burgundy reds and exquisite champagne. Symon was so polite (as was his usual self) and said, 'Um, actually no, this one is from Bordeaux. I do hope you like it.'

During that weekend I would arrive in the house kitchen before 7 a.m. My first and most important job was to turn on the coffee machine and fill the kettle for the early risers. Next, open the terrace doors to welcome in the morning air and soft sunshine then empty the dishwashers—quietly.

Breakfast was an informal buffet and simple. I just laid everything out on the dining table. It was all very delicious and appetising—hard cheese, perfect rounds of goat's cheese with a little pot of local honey, all served on a wooden board; platters of Serrano ham ribbons; bowls of plump, sweet fresh berries; plates of freshly sliced fruit and a large jar of homemade muesli. A jug of orange juice was chilling and I filled a colourful, wide-mouthed tureen with ice to keep the glass bottles of organic yoghurt cool until everyone was ready to eat. Butter curls sat ready on little dishes in the fridge. Once all the crockery and cutlery were set out, coffee and tea cups ready, I'd jump in the car and fly down the hill to our *boulangerie*, giving a friendly wave to Robert across the road who was often out early, watering his garden.

My basket was soon full of baguettes, mini croissants, *pains aux raisins* and other mouthwatering pastries to add to the continental breakfast. The tantalising smell of them sitting beside me in the passenger seat was often too much and I'd break off the end of a baguette, chewing contentedly during my short drive back.

With everything ready, I'd slip back to the cottage and have a quick breakfast before starting the watering of the garden and pots. A couple of hours later, it was time to clear away the remains of breakfast. There really was very little to do as everyone was so helpful. Once the dishwashers were on, I'd turn my attention to whatever lunch was to be, and so each day progressed until I'd stacked the last dessert plates in the dishwasher. I'd say goodnight and leave everyone to enjoy their wine and coffees and retire to my little haven to have a late cup of tea, check my emails or maybe watch a bit of TV to unwind before I fell into bed.

On the Saturday, everyone went off to Château de Salettes for lunch. There were now 14 of them and it was far easier for both guests and the restaurant (and me) to have a set menu to order from. Château de Salettes is a beautiful hotel and has kept its original stone façade but modernised the interior. The dining room matched that of any five-star hotel and I'd been told the suites were beautifully renovated.

Dinner back at Combe de Merigot that night was a barbecue. Symon had been down to the butcher in Gaillac and ordered Toulouse sausage and fillet steak. I was on the salads and to compensate for the lack of the usual carbohydrates, I put together a lentil salad with red onion, sun-dried tomatoes, feta, cherry tomatoes, fresh mint and basil and a basic dressing. A platter of blanched baby carrots, tossed in a little butter and toasted cumin seeds, plus a warm green bean, basil and pine nut salad added to the leafy green one, completed the feast. All this was followed by yet more cheese. I was under strict instructions from the boss that there was to be no dessert.

Symon was grinning, almost rubbing his hands together in anticipation when he'd asked, 'What's for dessert tonight, Annemarie?'

'Oh, um, sorry there isn't any. I *am* sorry, Symon. Didn't Mary tell you? She said you would all have had plenty today at the restaurant and not to bother,' I explained. His eyes widened.

'What? No dessert? Oh, PLEASE! Mary? Mary? Where are you?'

I quickly got out of the firing line but as I was on full dinner the following night, I managed to have Symon's ear when I was finishing up.

'Would you like a pavlova tomorrow night? Kiwi style?' I teased. His huge grin was all the answer I needed.

On Sunday morning, our generous fishing guest insisted he do brunch. He sharpened one of the big kitchen knives and with a chef's precision, finely sliced his incredible Alaskan salmon, complementing it with a pile of soft scrambled eggs, adding wild chives from the garden. It all looked so delicious accompanied with toasted sourdough slices.

While a sour cream lemon cake was still warm from the oven, I delivered it over to the house for afternoon tea. Lots of happy noises came from the table as everyone forked up mouthfuls in between sips of tea and coffee.

On the guests' last evening, I needed to use up whatever was left in the fridge as I hated wasting food. I made the same duck pâté canapés but I also created Roquefort puffs with the ends of the blue cheese and store-bought puff pastry, cutting out little rounds of it, baking them then when cool, dropping a small teaspoon of crumbled blue cheese on one piece and popping another on top to create a lid. I slid them back in the oven to warm through and to let the blue cheese melt a little. They really were delicious and so quick to make and went down very well. I'd prepared gazpacho for an entrée but one of the guests brought *escargots* (snails) as a gift so these became the entrée instead. I was asked more than once if I'd like to try one as they were so delicious. I politely declined. *Escargots* and frogs' legs are something I *never* wish to try. The mere thought of them makes me gag.

After the *escargots* I served a pretty salad of mangetouts, fresh peas, rocket and cherry tomatoes with slices of mozzarella, all drizzled with a balsamic dressing. The main was asparagus and lemon risotto with parmesan stirred through it and more parmesan shavings and lemon zest on top. At our market I'd found baby green and yellow round and short-length courgettes. I blanched these and just before serving, warmed them in a little olive oil in the pan and tossed the lot in fresh basil pesto topped with freshly torn basil. The colours looked so vibrant.

The fabulous cheeses followed and the pavlova rounded dinner off. I made sure this was distinctly New Zealand, with kiwifruit on top of the cream, and added strawberries and toasted slivered almonds. Symon was tickled pink and even Mary ate seconds which was the highlight of the evening for me.

By Monday lunchtime we were down to six guests and it was all very casual and easy. Plenty of cold meat and Toulouse sausage were left over from the barbecue so I made up a green salad, oven-roasted the rest of the cherry tomatoes and tossed them in the remaining pesto. The chilled gazpacho, served in crystal whisky glasses and topped with cubed avocado, croutons and a sprinkling of torn basil, looked so good. Everyone polished off the remains of the lemon cake with coffee then rose from the table groaning, swearing they weren't going to have dinner that night and would need to be fasting for the next week, having eaten and drunk so much over the past three days. As I loaded the dishwashers in the scullery, I stood grinning like a fool at the wall and punched the air—mission accomplished!

Mid-afternoon, after many hugs, kisses and thank yous, the last six guests departed. I waved until they'd disappeared over the crest of the drive and through the gate. Silence reigned. I stood for a moment, taking a couple of deep breaths, absentmindedly stroking the dogs' heads. They trotted beside me into the cottage and I put the kettle on for a cup of tea then fell on the couch with Indy tucked into my side. I put my feet up, waiting for the kettle to boil, and promptly fell asleep. Bliss.

I was sitting at Mary and Symon's dining table, typing up my blog while tantalising aromas washed over me, making me salivate. Two salmon and dill quiches were in the oven, using up leftover smoked salmon. Once done, the quiches would go in the freezer, ready for a casual lunch the following week when Mary, her son and his girlfriend arrived with some friends. The house needed minimal cleaning as I'd given it a thorough going-over before the weekend and it would only need a light dust and vacuum and, of course, the bedrooms and bathrooms done.

The dogs were now my constant companions, lounging in their basket next to me, but Indy made sure she kept one eye open just in case I got up from the table. She couldn't help herself. If I moved, she would instantly rise and follow me, even if it was only into the scullery. Poor girl. She needed lots more snuggling and cuddles without the family. Both dogs were lost for a few hours after everyone left and the house settled into its solitude and quiet.

I was still at the table when Tilly and Indy suddenly leapt up, skidded across the floor, barking their heads off and flying out through the French doors. A jet streaked across the sky, seemingly at treetops height, creating a colossal roar. There was a military base near Montauban and every now and then the jets would catapult over us. It was incredibly thrilling. Several weeks earlier, one flew at such a speed it created a sonic boom. Hearing the deafening crack, I'd thought something was crashing through the roof of the cottage and I'd found myself cowering in the kitchen, so frightened. I was told it's illegal for the military to do this in peacetime and I was sure there would have been complaints from the residents of the Tarn and its surrounds. The neighbours talked about it for weeks afterwards.

Calm resumed and the dogs padded quietly back in, climbed into their basket and promptly went to sleep, excitement over.

My day had been one of cooking and finishing off all the laundry and making a start on the ironing. It would take a few days to complete, with so many beds having been slept in. Mary was certainly not your usual employer and had already put some of the sheets and towels through the washing machine. The cleaning of all the bathrooms, vacuuming and re-making of beds would follow, ready for the next wave of family and visitors. I wasn't complaining because it was such an easy house to look after and work in. It was only a matter of being organised.

The long weekend with a full house had gone off well. My previous two weeks of hard graft, along with the planning and preparation of menus, had paid off. I was tired, but it was a good tired. For four days I'd been up at 6:30 a.m. to get myself ready, lay out breakfast on the buffet, shop, cook and help with lunch or do lunch myself. After dinner and the dishes, I'd fall into bed around 10:30 p.m. Sometimes I was unable to sleep as I was still hyper after an evening on the go. The first night after everyone left, I was tucked up in my bed with the light out by 9 p.m., sleeping solidly through until the sun's early morning fingers woke me.

During that long weekend, I'd had fun and it was easy to be amongst all the guests. You know I mean on the periphery. I was still an employee and needed to keep that uppermost in my mind while being friendly and welcoming. Not once, though, was I treated like staff. The guests and family were so complimentary about the food and all were very charming and relaxed. During their stay there was lots of banter about the possibility of me going to run one couple's home in Naples, Florida. Another asked could she please pack me in her suitcase and take me back to Scotland. It was just a bit of nonsense but was flattering and funny. Mary was having none of it!

Some of the conversations I overhead were just hilarious— unable to be repeated, of course. It was difficult to stifle my laughter as I went back and forth between the table, the kitchen and scullery. One particular evening the conversation became rather risqué. It was getting harder and harder to keep a straight face and pretend I hadn't heard. After one particularly naughty bit of chat, Symon followed me into the scullery to open another bottle of wine. He turned to me with a wicked grin on his face and asked, 'So did you hear that, Annemarie? They're outrageous!' All I could do was kick the door shut behind me and put my hand over my mouth, trying to muffle my laughter with Symon snorting beside me, trying to hold his laughter back, too. By the time the cheese and port were passed around, they were beyond the norms of dinner table etiquette and I gave up pretending I couldn't hear and giggled my way around the table.

A couple of days later, Ruth and I met up in Villemur to have coffee in the sunshine down by the Tarn. It'd been a while since we'd caught up with each other as she, too, had been busy with her catering work.

'What a great long weekend it was at Merigot, Ruth.' We sat down to chat and drink our coffee at Café Saint Jean after our lovely stroll through the town. 'It was a lot of work but great fun, too. Everyone was so nice and relaxed,' I said. 'Don't you think, when you're on holiday in beautiful surroundings, having fun with your friends, all your food and wine seems to taste that much better?'

'Absolutely,' Ruth agreed. 'I've just finished two catering jobs over the weekend and people were raving about the canapés. I did think to myself "what was all the fuss about?" but was very glad they enjoyed my food.'

It was fun to get away from our usual café haunts and for me to have the opportunity to dispense with some of my 10,000 words a day...

30

Full Circle

All four seasons in the French countryside had intersected my life, each one having its unique beauty. The golden wheat was now being harvested and the air was often thick with its dust. Huge trucks, piled high with hay bales, thundered along the roads, creating even more dust as bits flew off. Other fields filled the senses, with endless waves of yellow sunflowers, sometimes vivid red with poppies, and other times leafy green vines, heavy with grapes or purple with lavender. The days were long and hot and it was difficult to achieve much after lunch although it was cool working within the thick stone walls of the house. The afternoons were drowsy with oppressive low skies, stagnant air and the drone of insects. I pulled the shutters in to a crack so only a little light entered. Keeping the heat out was a priority.

In our cottage, the bedroom windows sat under the hangar. By 10 p.m. the heat build-up under the roofline was immense. After I'd made the mistake at the beginning of summer of leaving windows open all day, I learnt to let the morning air circulate and then closed them up. It helped but I would still be tossing and turning on the sheet during the hot nights, trying to find a cool place to rest.

Often I resorted to a cool shower in the wee hours and

would flop back into bed with water still clinging to me. Floating in the pool before bed also helped. One sweltering night, I turned the pool lights on and slipped into the water while the robot cleaning the pool was still circulating. It was up at the far end and I was at the other, wading through the water in the dusky evening light and watching lizards darting about on the rear brick wall. All of a sudden, something brushed against my leg and I screamed. Of course it was only the robot but I swear that thing must have had a sensor on it. It chased me around the pool and the *Jaws'* movie theme kept running through my head. I knew it was silly of me but it was a bit spooky. It was 10 p.m., almost dark and the robot's tail thing flipped up every now and then, squirting water. It was almost like it was alive.

With the heat came stormy weather. Siobhan, Doug and their friends Fabienne and Fabien (known to all as the Fabs) came over with their families for an evening barbecue and to cool off with a swim. After dinner, heavy black clouds thickened and clashed and there was the most tremendous thunder and lightning. The younger children scurried to their mothers. Some of us were in the pool as zigzag lightning lit up the sky followed by the most deafening thunderclap right overhead. All the lights went out; the heavens opened and the rain came down in sheets. That was the end of the fun evening. The older kids leapt out of the pool, with Fabien and me close behind. Siobhan rushed to turn on her phone torch to guide everyone. Even I was spooked. As we sheltered in the summer dining room, I managed to light some candles but the kids were upset and wanted to go home. It was all a bit much for them.

'Don't stay here on your own with the power out, Annemarie. Why don't you grab some overnight things and follow us home?' Siobhan kindly suggested.

'That's sweet but truly, I'll be fine, thanks. Bruno and Anne are just up the road if I need them. Anyway, I've got the dogs to look after and I can't bring them with me to yours. You've got

Boris there and it would be bedlam with my two. Look, it's stopped raining now. Go on, you all get going. The kids have had such a fright.'

Fabienne's youngest was still crying as she tried to calm him and bundle him in the car simultaneously.

'Get them home, Fabienne,' I said. 'They'll settle once you're on your way.'

'Yes, he's just got a fright; he'll be alright,' she agreed, kissing me on the cheeks. 'Thanks for a lovely evening.'

I waved to Fabien, already at the wheel, as Fabienne got in her side and they headed up the drive.

'I'll turn the car around and point the headlights on the pool gate and the cottage.' Doug jumped in their car. 'You'll be able to lock up and get the dogs out for a last pee before we go.'

'Thanks, Doug. I won't be long. Let me just grab the torch from the laundry and light a couple of candles inside, too.'

I flew inside and got myself sorted, calling the dogs once I was organised.

With the torch on, candles lit and the dogs by my side, I felt a lot happier. Doug and Siobhan were patiently sitting in the car with the children, waiting for me to finish. I leant in Doug's window.

'You all head off. Seriously, I'm absolutely fine. Text me when you're home. I want to know you're there safely and you can check that I'm tucked up OK, too. That alright? Night, kids. I'll see you soon,' I said, blowing kisses to them in the back seat.

'Yes, we'll do that,' Siobhan promised. 'I'll also check on you in the morning. Thanks for a super evening. Sorry it ended so abruptly.'

When the power wasn't back on in the morning, I called Bruno.

'Sorry to bother you, Bruno. The power went out last night in that brief storm. Could you call the power company for me? It will be torture for both me and the person on the end of the phone if I ring.' Bruno laughed.

'Wait in. I'll be there in a minute.' He clicked off.

Moments later I saw Bruno's van sitting at the gates at the top of the drive as he fiddled with something behind one of them. Instantly the power was back on. Two minutes later he was at the cottage door.

'That was quick!' I said, amazed. 'What did you do?'

'Flicked the fuse switch.' He gave me a wry smile. 'You could've done that last night, straight after it went off.'

If only I'd known, I would've got Doug to do it on their way home.

'Well, I'll know for next time, won't I, Bruno?' I felt foolish. 'It's a bit scary out here in the countryside with no power all night. Thank you so very much for coming up and sorting it out. Can I make you a cup of tea?'

'No, Annemarie, thank you.' He rattled his car keys. 'I need to get out in the vines as soon as possible. Anne's already made a start before the heat builds up. We'll see you soon. Come down and have a drink with us one evening next week?'

With arrangements made for that drink, he was out of the door, getting back to the never-ending work at his vineyard. Thank goodness for Bruno. I would need him again for a far more frightening incident before I left Combe de Merigot.

Steve had been gone for nine weeks, beavering away at work, back in the Auckland winter. It would be another five before we met up again in London. I was having guilt pangs for the lovely time I was enjoying. It seemed horribly unfair that he was missing the long summer days and evenings, as well as everything else that summer brought to the French country towns and villages. There were endless fêtes on with food, wine and music. Everyone was able to enjoy outdoor *apéros*, lunches and dinners with friends and family.

I was very fortunate to be invited to so many occasions and events. Similarly, I was having people over to our cottage, in between the family visits. The markets and towns were bustling with tourists and the local supermarket car park was often full of campervans when I went down. Summer living was vastly different from winter, that was for sure.

Ruth and Malc were amazing hosts and often invited people in for weekend lunches and dinners. Sometimes they chose to do it all themselves but usually everyone contributed something and you certainly never arrived without wine in your hand. I was the spare wheel at most gatherings but it really didn't matter to them and certainly didn't bother me. Several other women lived alone in the area so there was never any nonsense about not having a partner.

Lunch at Ruth and Malc's was always memorable, just because it was great fun with lots of laughter, interesting people and so relaxed. It was at one of their lunches that I met Bridget and Richard (Ruth's cousin), an English couple with a home in Brens, on the other side of Gaillac. I knew the area well as this was where Steve and I had first worked when we arrived in France. Such a shame I hadn't met them back then. We got on famously and while exchanging phone numbers, Bridget invited me down for coffee the following week.

Richard had told me all about their renovation of Pendaries Bas, a three-bedroomed house which they'd gutted, redoing it to how they wanted to live—as a family home rather than a holiday home.

I arrived for morning tea just as Bridget was finishing teaching a macaron cooking class.

'Welcome to Pendaries, Annemarie.' Bridget came to the kitchen doorway, drying her hands on a tea towel. She and Richard walked out to meet me as I crossed the courtyard and we exchanged kisses.

'*Bonjour.* Thank you so much for having me. What a super home you have. It's so pretty.' I looked up, admiring the green shutters. The house was a typical rectangular shape, two storeyed and built in the warm and solid, creamy local stone. It sat back on the section with the pool and paved outdoor seating area and well-kept garden, perfectly aligned with the house.

'Thank you very much. Yes, we love it. Come in and meet everyone. They've just finished making macarons and have done a grand job. You'll be able to sample some if you like,' Bridget volunteered. 'I've just put the kettle on. Coffee?'

'Super, yes, I'd love coffee, thanks.' I stepped into the kitchen where Bridget introduced me to her pupils. The macarons looked so inviting. Bridget had used various pastel colours in pretty shades of mauve, pink, lemon and baby blue.

'Richard, can you take the tray out to the table please?' Bridget was busy dispensing coffee grounds into the cafetière. 'I'll bring this out separately. Ladies, do follow Richard to the outdoor table and make yourselves comfortable.' Bridget nodded us out through the door.

We spent an enjoyable hour chatting and drinking coffee under the big umbrella, hiding from the glaring rays of the sun. Bridget proudly took me on a tour of the house. Brian, who built our cottage at Combe de Merigot, had done a superb job on Pendaries and the place was so well set up for their family, grandchildren and friends to come and stay. Every room was elegantly and tastefully furnished and one of the bedrooms housed Bridget's parents' marriage bed. After a look around the garden, I made my farewells and headed for home. I saw a lot of Bridget and Richard while living at Combe de Merigot, meeting up at various lunches and dinners and sharing Richard's birthday with them and Ruth at a wonderful terraced restaurant in Albi called Le Bruit en Cuisine, overlooking the cathedral.

Bridget is one of those multi-talented women—an artist, *pâtissière* (pastry chef), accomplished seamstress (you could wear her clothes inside out) and cook. I'd never seen such a collection of cookbooks as I did at her English home several years later, and that was after she'd culled them. On one occasion when we stayed with them for a significant birthday for Richard, Bridget created a stunning croquembouche-styled cake from 250-plus individual macarons she'd made instead of using the traditional profiteroles.

When Combe de Merigot was available as a holiday home before Mary and Symon owned it, Richard had booked the place out for family and friends for one of his milestone birthdays, arranging for caterers to come in to create a special dinner. Both proclaimed it to be one of the best weeks of their lives.

31

Carrying On

Malc took over Steve's role of head gardener, maintenance man, chauffeur, vehicle groomer, pool boy and general factotum. He was fluent in French and dealt with any French tradesmen for me—an absolute godsend. I asked him where he'd learnt the language and was so surprised to hear that it was by listening and imitating. He teased that he'd developed his accent after watching Inspector Clouseau (*Pink Panther* series) and the hilarious *'Allo 'Allo!* TV programmes. I was so glad to have Malc and Ruth in our lives. They'd become such great friends and were practical and fun with no airs and graces. Sometimes Ruth came to Combe de Merigot, too, to lend a hand. She whizzed around the lawns on the ride-on mower while Malc got on with hedges, ditches, the pool and anything else that needed doing. No working day ever began without the prerequisite cup of tea at my kitchen table. At least twice a week, around 8 a.m., there would be a knock at my door.

'Morning, boss,' Malc would holler, coming through the door, often with pastries in hand, still warm from the *boulangerie*. 'I'll put the kettle on, shall I?' He was already at the kitchen sink, filling the kettle, grinning over his shoulder at me as I came into the kitchen. There was no need to reply. 'Right, show me today's list then,' he'd say, reaching across the table to grab it from me, almost sending our cups flying. 'Geez, you're a demanding woman,' Malc would tease, reading through what needed doing. As we drank our tea, we chatted through the priorities for the day and any gossip, events and goings-on around our neighbourhoods.

'I'd better get this down me and get on if I'm to get through half this list,' Malc would joke, standing and draining the last of his tea, thumping the empty mug down on the bench top. 'See you at morning tea, missus.' He'd stride out the door, pulling his hat low to shade against the sun.

There were times when Malc was called back to the UK, which meant he couldn't always fit in the work at Combe de Merigot. I needed the help so he called in reinforcements in the form of his good friend, John. What a 'long drink of water' that man was at 1.95 metres tall and so slim, too. He and his wife, Jenny, kindly opened their door to me and invited me to their home several times for dinner and drinks.

John was an experienced and passionate gardener and being ex-Royal Air Force, he liked to see a military precision to all he did. The first job he tackled was the storeroom, which looked like a bomb site. Both Malcolm and I were guilty of flinging tools, hoses and the associated gardening paraphernalia in through the door, instead of putting everything back in its rightful place. Just as well Steve wasn't there to see the disorder. Since he'd been gone, this, too, became a dumping ground for unwanted goods. I did explain to John that Steve hadn't left it that way.

By the time John finished, the storeroom was pristine and would've passed any air chief marshal's inspection. You could've eaten off that concrete floor. He brought a trailer in and carted all the rubbish off to the dump, oiled and sharpened the tools and systematically shelved or hung everything in perfect symmetry. It was only then that John felt able to work properly. There were some days I almost stood to attention and half raised my arm to salute as he marched up the drive for his mid-morning cuppa with such a straight back.

John, too, got into the pattern of picking up a couple of croissants from the *boulangerie* on his way to the 'office'. I was always well and truly up and ready before either he or Malc arrived at the door wanting a hot brew before the onslaught of the day as the girls needed to be let out for their morning toileting. If I wasn't, I'd open the laundry door to find a puddle and a little deposit. It only happened a couple of times in the winter when Tilly wasn't too happy being hurried out of the door last thing at night before bed.

With our cuppas done and dusted, we'd disperse to perform our various functions. As I always made a coffee mid-morning for myself, I'd make one for the boys, and Ruth if she was there. We'd find a shady spot or sit in the summer dining room and have this together. It felt like we were a team, working to maintain this beautiful property. They were just as proud of the place as I was. There was never a lot of time to get lonely as there was plenty of company if I wanted it and I came to enjoy the solitude when I did have it. Often during the week, though, Denise or I would ring each other, saying, 'I've got more than enough for two for dinner; come over.' We shared a few of these evenings, enjoying good food, good wine and plenty of chat.

Cousin Catherine arrived from Banbury in the UK to stunning weather. We toured the countryside early morning to beat the heat of the day, returning home for a late lunch. Our visits took in Cordes-sur-Ciel, the Albi Cathedral and the Toulouse-Lautrec Museum and gardens. We included a little retail therapy as well as a late-afternoon visit to Puycelsi. She enjoyed most afternoons poolside, reading her book and dozing, with intermittent dips in the water while I got on with my work.

Denise and I took Catherine to one of the many summer

apéro concerts held in the garden of the 10th-century Abbey St Michel in Gaillac which sits right on the River Tarn and has terrific views from the rear garden. Local vineyards bring their wine along for tasting. For a €5 entry fee, you receive tickets for two glasses of whatever takes your fancy and a little plate of olives, meats and crisps, plus the joy of live music. The tables were set out cheek by jowl, some with sun umbrellas, so as many people as possible could fit in and enjoy the evening.

I loved watching the couples up dancing, some holding each other quite formally, children skipping in and out of the tables and everyone chatting in the late sunshine. It was often hot and sticky in the evenings and many women arrived back at their tables, dabbing at shiny red faces with a tissue, the men mopping beads of sweat from their own brows. Denise and I had fun at several of these concerts held over the summer in different locations around the Tarn.

Early June, I got a call from her.

'Hello, girlfriend, it's me,' Denise sang. I could hear her smiling into the phone.

'Hello, me. What's happening?'

'Well, what's your diary like for the 14th of July?'

'Stand by. I'll have a look.' I grabbed my diary off the kitchen table. 'I'm free as a bird. Hey, it's Bastille Day. Shall we do something?' I suggested.

'You're too late. It's all organised. You're coming to dinner with me and six others to Auberge du Pont Vieux. It's a fabulous little restaurant in Albi, right by the old bridge. Every year Sally and John have a standing booking for a table for eight on Bastille night so we can watch the fireworks from there at 10:30 p.m. They've asked if you'd like to join us,' Denise explained.

'Sounds fantastic. I'd love it. Book me in.'

I'd met Sally and John several times at drinks at Denise and Ian's. They were a very relaxed and lovely couple and I'd enjoyed spending time with them.

'You're going to love the place as the food's excellent and

there's a dining parapet overlooking the Tarn River. The restaurant itself has a small dining room and is on the other side of the road. Over the summer, though, they set up on the parapet and waiters run back and forth, dodging the traffic as they go. Well, that's a bit of an exaggeration. It's a fairly quiet street but it's rather fun to watch them with laden dinner plates stacked up their arm, trotting across the road to serve the guests. And the fireworks afterwards go on for a full half hour. It's an amazing night.'

'I'm really excited now. Please say thanks to Sally and John for the invitation. That will be a Bastille Day to remember. Wonderful!'

The date duly rolled around and John, Sally and Denise arrived at my door to collect me. I ran out to join them.

'Hello, everyone.' I climbed into the backseat and leant over to kiss Denise on the cheek. 'I'm so looking forward to this evening. Thank you, Sally and John, for inviting me.' From the back I gave them a little rub on their shoulders to say hello instead of a kiss.

'*Bonsoir*,' they both chimed.

'You're very welcome. Glad you could come with us,' Sally said. 'You'll love it. It's always a great evening.'

'All set? Locked in?' John checked in the rearview mirror, ready to set off up the drive.

'Good to go, thanks.' I fastened my seatbelt and tucked my handbag in beside me.

The restaurant was abuzz as the waiter led us across the road to our table on the terrace, where we joined the rest of our group. Kisses exchanged and introductions made, everyone sat down and placed their drink orders. Half an hour later, I excused myself so I could go and stand at the old stone wall to enjoy the view of the ancient bridges and the city of Albi, directly across the water. What a gorgeous setting.

The restaurant parapet sits between the two most historic bridges in Albi; Le Pont Vieux (The Old Bridge) can be dated back to the 1200s and is still in service, and the other is Le Pont Neuf (The New Bridge) built in 1868. A savage battle took place there on August 22, 1944, between the Resistance and German forces.

I had to drag myself away when John beckoned me as the first course was on the table. It was a set menu and each course was a work of art, beautifully presented and delicious. After some amuse-bouches, we ate baked sea bass fillet, saffron risotto and candied peppers followed by hazelnut lamb with mesclun salad. By the time the lamb was served, I was struggling to finish. However, I soldiered on and did also manage to consume the delicious dessert of strawberry and lime sorbet, limoncello baba and strawberry whipped cream.

It was a warm and balmy evening and all of us women were in sleeveless dresses. The light was beginning to fade and the bridges and roads rapidly filled with spectators as the clock ticked closer to 10:30 p.m. People on Le Pont Vieux jostled for prime position to get the best view of the fireworks. The noise level increased and the excitement was palpable. Those of us on the restaurant parapet leant up against the old stone wall, watching and waiting. We had the best fireworks' viewing spot in town.

They began with the most deafening bang with bursts of colourful, showering, sparkling lights and went on for a full half hour. There were comments from other diners about the state of the French economy and how a lot of taxpayer's money was going up in smoke all over France. Not my place to comment but for me they were the best fireworks I'd ever seen.

32

More Socialising

After an early dinner in Ruth and Malcolm's garden, a fun group of us (Italian, American, Parisian, English and me, the New Zealander) travelled in convoy to Café Joubert in Fayssac. The conversation at dinner had been lively and interesting with the diversity of cultures and viewpoints. Café Joubert was a very popular venue in the village and hosted musicians from all over the world so it was hard to get to the bar and get a seat. That night it was a New Orleans-style guitarist. He really belted out the numbers and although it wasn't my style of music, it was a great evening.

It was getting late and I was conscious the dogs had been inside for quite a few hours. I said my farewells, kissing everyone goodbye. Last were Malc and Ruth and they stepped outside with me so we could hear ourselves speak.

'Now, when you get to the bottom of the hill, turn right then first left. You'll see the signs to Gaillac and the roads will become familiar to you,' Malcolm instructed.

'OK, got it.' I slung my bag over my shoulder and turned to go.

'And for heaven's sake, don't forget to text us to tell us you're safely home. Got it?' He pointed his finger at me. I felt like I was their teenage daughter.

'Yes, yes, Malc, I will. Now I have to go. The dogs will be bursting.'

I couldn't quite believe that in my mid-50s, I would be driving very late at night, down French country roads in the pitch black, finding my way home. Nor could I believe I was living by myself on a large estate in the French countryside. If you'd asked me 18 months ago if that would be me, I would've looked at you, shocked, thinking you quite mad. I was learning more and more exactly what I was capable of. For that brief time, I relished the independence and only having to look after myself after 25 years of taking care of a family.

I attended many social events by myself, as did other women. It certainly didn't bother me and I was always welcomed on arrival. One that particularly stands out in my mind is the annual Fêtes Musicales I went to at Castelnau-de-Montmiral as it was magical. It has a respected reputation and when I arrived, the community centre was bursting with people from local and far-flung places. The talent of the performers was extraordinary and one twenty-something young woman sent shivers down my spine with a copy-cat rendition of one of Adele's songs, 'Someone Like You'. Another was a twelve-year-old boy who played Mozart on the piano. It sounded perfect, not that I would've known if he made a mistake.

One exceptionally hot day, Karen and Ian, friends from Auckland, arrived for a visit. They were touring France and sharing an apartment with another couple in Cordes-sur-Ceil for a week. They drove down to me at Merigot to have lunch and a swim, escaping the heat and throngs of people at the Saint-Antonin-Noble-Val market. It was fantastic to see them and to hear all that was happening in our village back in Auckland.

After a tour of the house and our cottage, we sat down to eat in the summer dining room. The afternoon disappeared with all of us dipping in and out of the pool and talking leisurely. Tilly and Indy lay in the shade, panting in the heat but wanting to be part of the socialising, too.

'What a heavenly place to work and live, Annemarie.' Karen sighed, giving an expansive sweep of her arm, taking in the pool and the summer dining room. 'You definitely landed on your feet here.'

'It truly is and yes, we were very fortunate. This is exactly what I envisaged when we first applied for the job at Tristan and Richard's place all those months ago,' I reminisced, leaning back in my chair. We were quiet for a minute, both of us deep in thought. Ian was lying back in one of the loungers with his eyes closed, soporific in the drowsy heat of the afternoon.

'You know, Karen, it's been a privilege to be part of caring for this place,' I continued. 'It's a special lifestyle and doesn't really feel like a job. We couldn't have wished to work for better people. From the start they've shown us respect and have been so good to us. I'm going to miss them.' I murmured the last words, almost to myself, realising the truth of it.

Ian roused himself and wandered over to the dogs, giving them both a scratch behind the ears. 'Time to go, Karen,' he announced, looking at his watch. 'It's 6 p.m. and the others will be wondering where we've got to.' Ian stretched and yawned. 'I could get used to living like this,' he said, looking around him.

Karen snorted and stood up. 'In your dreams!'

Ian made me laugh as we'd all love to get used to living life at Merigot. It was idyllic.

During the week, I went to Cordes to have dinner with them and their friends. It was yet another stunning, hot summer's evening and we sat out on the terrace under the shady arbour of a wisteria vine. Our view was green pastures and razed, corn-coloured fields now the sunflowers had been harvested. Ruler-straight lines of trees and hedges intersected the fields, creating a marvellous patchwork. Brightly coloured hang-gliders passed so low over the top of us, they called *bonsoir* as they made the most of the fabulous weather and light breeze.

I was at the bench making a sandwich when I saw Malc crunching across the gravel courtyard towards the cottage. A sharp rap and his head appeared around the doorway.

'Got a minute?' he asked.

'Sure, what's up?'

'Hear the tractor up in the vines?'

I nodded.

'It's Monsieur Ferrand mowing up there. He's asking about you.' Malc nodded his head at me, grinning.

'Really? What about me?'

'He wants to know if you're the New Zealander he's heard about. So I told him yes. He'd like to ask you something about his granddaughter who's travelling around Australia and soon to be in New Zealand. I told him you were going back soon. Just come with me and talk with him… Don't worry. I'll translate for you. I doubt whether you'll catch much as he's from around here.'

'Right, hang on.' I was curious what he could possibly want me for but washed my hands, quickly drying them before we went out.

As we approached the vines, Monsieur Ferrand saw us, shut down the tractor and stepped down to meet us, removing his hat at the same time.

'*Bonjour*, Monsieur Ferrand. *Je suis* Annemarie.' I smiled at him, extending my hand.

He wiped one hand on the back of his trousers then gently shook mine.

'*Bonjour, madame.*'

Malc took over from there as Monsieur Ferrand explained

why he wanted to talk to me. His granddaughter, Camille, and her boyfriend were currently in Australia working for their accommodation and meals but were having a rough time of it. Some people were taking advantage of them, having them sleep in a shed, not giving them an evening meal, that sort of thing. He was anxious about her. They were due in New Zealand in four weeks and he wondered if I would be happy to meet them. Poor Monsieur Ferrand needed to know Camille was OK.

'Malc, please assure Monsieur Ferrand,' I nodded, smiling into his anxious face, 'I'll be delighted to have them to stay. I'll look after them and feed them for a week if necessary.'

Malc explained all this to dear Monsieur Ferrand who quickly turned to one side, wiping his eyes but not before I'd seen them full of tears. He grabbed my hand, shaking it furiously.

'*Merci, madame, merci!*'

I left Malc with him while I nipped back to the cottage, grabbed pen and paper and filled it with all the New Zealand contact details Camille would need to get hold of me and took it back to Monsieur Ferrand. He couldn't stop beaming. I thought he was going to kiss me at one point.

Malc walked back down to the cottage with me.

'That's very kind of you, Annemarie. He was so grateful.'

I waved my hand dismissively.

'Not really. It's "paying it forward", isn't it? Siobhan and Doug took care of us when we needed help in a foreign country. I'll take care of Camille and her boyfriend in New Zealand. That's just as it should be. Besides, I'd like to think if one of our sons was having a tough time either at home or overseas, someone would take them under their wing and help.'

Camille and her boyfriend got in touch once I was back in New Zealand and we arranged a pickup time and place and I brought them home. What a delightful couple. It was hilarious as they thought they'd died and gone to heaven staying with us because I made sure I fussed over them, giving them good food, wine, running them around Auckland sightseeing and dropping them at the airport for their return flight to France. I couldn't have them bad-mouthing New Zealand to all and sundry in France, could I? It was an absolute pleasure and Steve and I both enjoyed their company and practising some French.

About a month later, a large box appeared at our front door. Inside was the most delicious French food—tins of our favourite lentils, confit duck, bonbons, macarons, a tea cosy with a print of Gaillac on it, tea towels and much more. While Camille and her boyfriend were with us, we'd talked about the markets and supermarkets and the food we enjoyed in France and Camille had remembered this. The box was a gift from her parents and grandparents, thanking us for taking care of Camille and her boyfriend. It was such a treat and so generous of them.

It was a wonderful reunion the following year when we were back in France and Camille invited us to lunch with her parents and grandparents. It was a fun time, with lots of interpretation needed.

An Awful Fright

After Steve left, I always made sure the cottage was locked when I was over at the house and locked the door behind me when I went indoors. I was so glad I was vigilant with this.

It was four days before I was due to leave Merigot; Mary and Symon had gone south for the day and wouldn't be returning until after dinner. While I was working upstairs in the main house that afternoon, the dogs started barking in the sitting room and I heard a car pull up outside. From a bedroom window, I saw a man get out. Someone I didn't recognise. He looked to be in his 40s, a little unkempt and furtive. I hesitated a few moments before I leant out of the open window and called down to him.

'Hello, can I help you?' He spun around and appeared surprised. He looked up to find where the voice had come from. My skin started to crawl. I didn't like the look of him at all.

'Ah, 'ello.' I knew at once he wasn't French but he wasn't English either. With swarthy features and black hair, he could've been any number of nationalities. It was the curl of his lip and rather cold and almost coal-black eyes that gave me an uneasy feeling.

'Are you the owner?' he asked with a strong accent and an insincere smile, revealing he had several teeth missing.

'No, I'm…we're the guardians here.' I didn't need him to know that I was on my own. 'Is there something I can help you with?' I asked, trying to sound confident.

'Perhaps.' He slid his hands into his pockets, casually looking around and taking his time to answer. 'I could see from the gate this was a very nice house. I'm looking for a place to hold a party. This would be a very nice place to party, yes? I am very interested. Can you come down so we can discuss it?' That creepy smile was back.

There was no way I was going outside to discuss anything with him. Thank God I'd locked the doors. How long had he been watching from the gate?

'I'm sorry but the owners don't rent out the property,' I told him in my coldest tone.

'Let me speak to your husband, yes? Where is he?' He turned, taking a cursory look around the garden. 'I don't see him. Is he in the house with you?' Again, that awful smile. I was now petrified and starting to shake.

'He's…he's helping a neighbour. I'll ring him.' The man just smirked. I could tell he didn't believe me. 'I've already told you, the owners don't rent the property out. I'm very sorry but you need to leave.' My voice had lost its confidence and so had I.

'I can wait until…your husband…arrives,' he mocked, now folding his arms and leaning back against the car bonnet.

'I'm ringing him right now.' I lifted my phone to show him and moved inside the room. With shaking hands I rang Bruno.

'Annemarie. *Bonjour, ca va?*' he boomed, picking up my call.

'Bruno, Bruno, there's a man here and he won't leave. He says he wants to rent the place for a party and I've told him that's not possible but he won't listen. Help me please!' I whispered desperately into the phone.

Bruno was immediately serious. 'Where are you? In the house? Are the doors locked?'

'Yes, yes, I am and they are. He said he'd wait for my husband. I told him he was helping a neighbour. He won't leave, Bruno. Can you come quickly and pretend you're Steve?' I pleaded.

'I'll be right there. Don't go outside.'

I returned to the window. The man was still there and now casually smoking, wandering around. I was terrified he'd try the door.

'My husband's on his way. He'll tell you exactly what I've told you,' I reported haughtily. From the window I could see Bruno's van racing through the gates, creating great clouds of dust in his haste to reach the house. 'Ah, here he is now.' My relief was enormous.

The man quickly turned to check, ground the cigarette out in the gravel and opened the car door, hurrying into the driver's seat. He was no longer self-assured and smirking.

Bruno's van came to a swift halt beside the man's car, making sure he wasn't blocking the driveway.

Bruno isn't a tall man but he certainly looked taller to me as he spoke.

'*Bonjour, monsieur*. I believe my wife has already told you the owners don't rent out the property. I would like you to leave now and not return. I took a photo of your vehicle and registration as I came down the drive. If you ever try to come back, I'll call the police immediately.' Bruno spoke quietly, hands on hips, looking the man directly in the eye. There was no mistaking his message.

Slamming the car door shut and turning the engine on, the man sneered at Bruno, muttered something inaudible and sent gravel flying as he raced up the drive.

I could hardly get down the stairs, my legs were shaking so much, but I made it outside and rushed over to Bruno, clutching his arm.

'Oh my God, Bruno! I was so frightened when he wouldn't leave. Thank goodness you were home. I should've called the police but I knew you'd be here quicker. What if he comes back? Mary and Symon won't be home until later tonight. This has never happened before.' The words tumbled out as I tried to get a grip on myself.

Bruno put his arm around my shoulders.

'You're OK now.' He patted my arm. 'He won't come back. I'd say he was a chancer, seeing if the place was empty and perhaps looking to burgle. He obviously got a fright finding you here but decided to become menacing, thinking you were on your own.' He was very calm and reassuring. 'It might be time for those gates to be automated. That way no one can come down the drive when you're here on your own.'

'Yes. I'll talk to Mary and Symon tomorrow. Thank you so much for coming. I'll be alright in a minute.' I gave Bruno a tentative smile, trying to sound stronger than I felt.

'Why don't you feed the dogs then lock up and come down to have a drink with us before dinner? Settle your nerves.' Bruno checked his watch. 'Anne will be coming in now. She'll want to have the kids' dinner ready soon.'

'Actually, I think I'll do that. Thanks, Bruno. I so appreciate you dropping everything.'

'No problem. Get yourself sorted and we'll see you shortly.' He jumped back in his van, turned and waved, heading back up the drive.

I couldn't wait for Mary and Symon to return so I at least had someone else on the property. For the first time ever, I took the dogs up to bed with me. Sleep, however, was impossible until I heard the Range Rover on the gravel and Mary and Symon's voices outside.

Hearing the car and their voices too, the dogs ran helter-skelter down the stairs, barking loudly. I let them out into the night to greet them. My unwanted visitor story could wait until the morning.

'My God, Annemarie, what a terrible fright you've had.'

Mary was horrified to learn next day about the strange man arriving at the house.

'I'll get those gates sorted as soon as I can.' Symon, too, was shocked. 'We need to advise the police and give them the car details and a description of the man. I'll call Bruno to get the information and the photo. I know you only have a few more days with us, Annemarie, but I can't have Mary staying over here on her own without the security of locked gates either. I don't want this happening again.'

He immediately went online, looking at various companies to call.

End of the Golden Weather...

Leaving France was a long process, given the three-month lead time to my departure. I had everything ready to be shipped home and only needed to complete the paperwork and call the shippers. The days suddenly flew by and it became a mad rush with dinners and lunches out and friends coming to me. Exactly the same as it was at the beginning of this adventure when we were leaving New Zealand, but now in reverse.

A special occasion was with Mary and Symon who took me to lunch at the Michelin-starred restaurant at Hotel Château de Salettes. It was a wonderful day. The food was superb; the wines to match were delicious and Mary and Symon's company entertaining. I loved it all. The interior was very elegant and modern; some would say minimalist but there were plenty of people dining and chatting to create a special atmosphere.

We talked and talked, enjoying the wines and taste sensations as course after course arrived, each interspersed with an amuse-bouche. Even though every portion was small and a work of art, we were all full and feeling a bit slow as we left the table.

'I'm going to have a little lie down, I think. Certainly no

need for dinner tonight,' Mary pronounced as she got out of the car at Merigot.

'Absolutely not,' I agreed, and a little burp escaped my lips while unlocking the cottage door. 'Oops, excuse me!' I laughed, my hand flying to my mouth. I turned to Mary and Symon. 'I'm still digesting all that wonderful food. Again, thank you so very much for such a super treat. I loved it all.'

My very last night at Combe de Merigot was even more special. Symon was quietly insistent *they* cook for *me*. It was a marvellous evening with the two of them, the double doors to the terrace wide open to the warm evening and Tilly and Indy happily ensconced in their baskets. Simple pleasures of delicious food and wine shared with good company.

Siobhan arrived early the next day to help me do a final clean of the cottage. By the time we'd finished and heaved my bags into the car, I was shattered, both physically and emotionally, and could only stand and look for the last time at the pond, the garden, the fields beyond and lastly that beautiful house that I had so loved. Siobhan's voice shook me from my reverie when she touched my arm.

'I'll wait in the car. Take your time. There's no hurry to leave.' Her eyes told me she knew exactly how I was feeling.

Mary and Symon came out to say goodbye. There was no prolonged farewell. I don't think I could've coped with it. They'd been amazing employers who I felt had become our friends. I thrust a card into Mary's hand which said everything I wanted to say to them. Both she and Symon had spoken to me so warmly about my time with them the night before. All that was left to do was give Indy and Tilly a quick kiss on their soft, furry heads, hug Mary and Symon and leave.

'Oh, Annemarie,' Mary said so quietly it was hardly audible. I couldn't speak. My throat was almost closed with emotion.

Siobhan had the car running and it was only moments before I joined her, pulling the door shut as we began rolling down the drive. I couldn't look back. I wouldn't have seen anything anyway, with eyes full of blinding tears. Much as I wanted to see Steve and everyone in New Zealand again, I felt an overwhelming sadness. We'd been incredibly happy at Combe de Merigot and the only reasons for us to leave were to take care of our financial future and be nearer to family.

I was fortunate to be having my last few nights in France staying with Doug, Siobhan and the children. As Doug came through the door after work that evening, he greeted me with a big hug and a grin on his face, booming, 'Hello, roomie.'

Denise came over to join us on my last night, as did Fabienne, and it was all a bit tearful saying goodbye. I was surprised and spoilt with gifts and cards. Fabienne gave me an exact copy of an orange, patent-leather bag she owned; one I'd admired on several occasions. Siobhan and Doug produced a lovely necklace to remember them by and Denise, a beautiful silver charm bracelet with each charm having a particular significance to our friendship. She'd been my soulmate, dinner companion and outings friend since Steve left and we'd had some great laughs and evenings together. These gifts were so very precious and full of memories.

It had been a busy summer. I was looking forward to no housework for a whole month and no washing, ironing and folding of the many sheets and pillowcases or towels, hand towels, and other linen that homes such as Combe de Merigot required. Having said that, it had always given me a great sense of satisfaction and pleasure to stand back and look in the enormous linen press and see shelf upon shelf of crisply ironed and stacked sheets, duvet covers and pillowcases and the towels all fluffy and perfectly folded. Everything was so white and pristine.

When I look back, none of it was ever a chore. I was fortunate to be working in a magnificent old home, surrounded by beautiful antiques, art and treasured objects with quality linens and fabrics everywhere. To have had such a kind, warm and generous family to work for was the icing on the cake.

It was an incredible experience and one I'll never forget. There were no regrets, even with the difficult months at Mas de Lavande. To have lived and worked in France and immerse ourselves in the life was my dream come true. Steve and I knew we would always return.

Most people we met had little but gave so much. Their doors and hearts were always open to us; there was a seat at their table and there was joy in the everyday life of sharing food, wine and time. I felt so changed by it all. This was the French way, a lifestyle I wanted to translate into our New Zealand life. Many English people had walked away from big-income jobs and a lot of stress in the UK to live a much simpler, more relaxed and less-moneyed lifestyle in France. The French we met had welcomed us into their homes and lives and I was thrilled to have experienced a true French life through them.

We hoped that over the coming years, our friends from France would come and stay with us. We could then reciprocate the amazing warmth and hospitality we'd received. Many said the journey to New Zealand would be too daunting for them though we Antipodeans think nothing of it. Bridget and Richard and one other couple were the only ones who would eventually make the trip to come and stay.

During our whole time in France, and particularly in my three months alone, I learnt an awful lot about myself. I already knew I got on well with most people but there were times I'd felt inadequate. Not anymore. Living alone as a mature woman, I got to know myself, what I was capable of and what I was good at. I learnt to rely on myself, enjoy being alone and discovered that, really, I was OK.

I'll never stop dreaming and planning 'what next?' If I do, you'll know I've stopped breathing.

My bag weighed 34 kilos, which the check-in man refused to accept. It was too heavy for the baggage handler, and for me and Doug. There we were, squatting on the floor next to check-in with my suitcase wide open, trying to remove at least two kilos. I busily stuffed shoes and clothes into my laptop bag and handbag. We managed it and €46 in overweight charges later, the luggage was checked in and on its way. And so was I, trying not to sniffle or sob too loudly so as not to disturb the man seated next to me. He sensibly slipped his headphones on and buried his head in his book.

On the ground at Heathrow, my first thought was, *Now how do I ask in French where I catch the coach to Oxford?* It took a moment for me to remember I was now back on English-speaking soil and didn't need to worry. The charming coach driver managed to heave my heavy suitcase into the hold, grunting, 'Where the 'ell 'ave you been, luv?' When I explained I was moving back to New Zealand, he snorted. 'Well, I definitely know you 'aven't left anyfink behind,' he said, standing and rubbing his lower back.

I was looking forward to seeing Steve again in a week's time back at Heathrow Airport. I did wonder if he was bracing himself for the onslaught of my 10,000-plus words a day...

Epilogue

Steve and I lived back in New Zealand for five years, returning to France three times, then did exactly the same thing again— put all our worldly possessions into storage, rented out the house and moved 12,000 miles, this time to London in March 2018, aged 60. You can read that story in *Late Life Adventures in London and Beyond*, due to be published in 2022.

Mary and Symon sold Combe de Merigot approximately 18 months after we left and have recently bought and renovated another property in a different area of France. We've become lovely friends though have yet to get to their new French home after several attempts and cancellations due to COVID-19 during 2020, but we met up with them often for museum visits, theatre, coffees and dinner at theirs while living in London.

Denise and Ian, too, eventually sold their home and have now moved to another European country to continue their lives. Domaine de Ménerque is now a boutique hotel.

Siobhan and Doug, Malc and Ruth and most others mentioned continue to enjoy their lives in France and we stay in touch frequently and see them each time we go.

Bridget and Richard had ten wonderful years going back and

forth to their French home, Pendaries Bas, before selling it. It was time for them to look for new holiday adventures.

Margot, Steve's sister, battled her cancer so bravely, undergoing stem cell transplant and more treatments. This extended her life for several years but she very sadly passed away in December 2017.

My darling friend Andy became unwell while we were with him and Emma in Dorset. It was an absolute tragedy he passed away the following year after a battle with cancer.

Map of the Area We Lived In

In *My French Platter*, we lived near Brens.

In *My French Platter Replenished*, we first lived in Lisle-sur-Tarn, then later, very close to Gaillac.

Message from the Author

Thank you so very much for reading my book and I hope you really enjoyed it. Please, please could you leave a review on Amazon and/or Goodreads? I would be extremely grateful as these reviews greatly influence potential readers and push books up the ranks.

The following recipes and others, as well as more detailed photos of Combe de Merigot, can be found on my website. I'd also love to have your comments and am happy to answer any questions so do please get in touch with me through:

Email: annemarierawson@gmail.com
Facebook: www.facebook.com/annemarie.rawson.1
Website: www.annemarierawson.com

If you enjoy reading memoirs, I recommend you pop over to the Facebook group We Love Memoirs to chat with other authors and me. They've been incredibly supportive of me, a novice and untrained writer, and are the friendliest and warmest group of people I've met. If you're thinking of writing your memoir and need help, get in touch with Victoria Twead, a very successful author and owner of Ant Press, the company that helped me publish my books, and Jacky Donovan, my editor. You couldn't wish for better expertise.

RECIPES

Simple Fig Chutney

Ingredients
13-15 fresh ripe figs
1 tbsp olive oil
2 red onions, thinly sliced
150 mls (5 fl oz) balsamic vinegar
100 mls (3 fl oz) red wine vinegar
300 g (10 oz) soft brown sugar
Zest and juice of one lemon
2 tsps mixed spice
10 g (⅓ oz) freshly grated root ginger
Salt and pepper

Method
Remove the stalk from the figs and cut into quarters.
Heat the oil in a large pan over medium heat and fry the onions
for five minutes until soft and slightly caramelised.
Add all the other ingredients to the pan except for the figs,
season with salt and pepper.
Bring to the boil.
Allow to simmer for 30 minutes.

Once the liquid has reduced to syrup, add the figs and cook for a further 15 minutes, stirring occasionally.
Pour into sterilised jars and allow to cool.

Pavarotti's Ham Glaze

I use this for our Christmas Day ham.

Ingredients
1 cooked, free-range ham on the bone
3 oranges (use Seville oranges, if available, or tangelos)
330 g (11 oz) runny honey
60 mls (2 fl oz) fresh orange juice
200 g (7 oz) brown sugar
2 tsp Dijon-style mustard
Cloves
Heavy-duty aluminium foil

Method
Peel the rind from the orange skin and cut it into short strips. In a small bowl mix the honey, orange juice, brown sugar and mustard.
Carefully strip the skin off the ham, trying not to disturb the layer of creamy fat beneath it. Score the surface of the fat into small diamond shapes and stud each diamond with a whole clove.
Line a large roasting tin with a double thickness of aluminium

foil, raising the foil above the edges of the tin. This will catch drips of glaze falling off the ham and prevent flare-ups in the oven. Place the ham in the tin, making sure the foil stays upright.

Pour the glaze over the ham and put the ham in an oven preheated to 225°C (440°F).

Mix the strips of orange peel in the glaze bowl, coating them with any remaining glaze. Spoon the orange strips over the top of the ham about halfway through glazing. It will take about 45 minutes. As parts of the fat take on enough colour, place small pieces of foil on top to deflect the heat.

If you want to serve the ham hot, allow an hour longer (1½ to 1¾ hours in total) to heat through, but lower the heat to 180°C (350°F) after one hour. You may need to protect the entire surface of the ham with foil after 50-60 minutes. Baste the ham with the glaze every 15 minutes.

Gazpacho

Ingredients for gazpacho
1 small red onion, peeled and chopped
1 slice day-old sourdough bread, crust removed and roughly chopped
24 cm (9") cucumber (telegraph if available)
400 g (14 oz) vine-ripened tomatoes
2-3 coriander (cilantro) roots, scrubbed and chopped
2 large cloves garlic, peeled and chopped
¾ tsp smoked sweet Spanish paprika
1¼ tsp salt
1½ tbsp extra virgin olive oil
1 medium red pepper, halved, deseeded, cored and finely chopped
1 tbsp Spanish sherry vinegar or red wine vinegar

Crouton topping
2 tbsp olive oil
2 slices day-old sourdough bread, cubed
Sea salt
1 perfectly ripe avocado
1 tbsp chopped fresh coriander

1 lime (or lemon) cut into small wedges

Method
Put onion in a bowl and pour on cold water to cover then soak
for 15 minutes.
Put the chopped bread in a shallow dish, cover with cold water
and soak for 15 minutes.
Peel cucumber, cut in half lengthways and scoop out the seeds
with a teaspoon. Discard seeds and chop flesh coarsely.
Drop tomatoes into a saucepan of boiling water, count to 15,
then drain and let the cold tap run over them until they feel
cool. Peel then cut into quarters and scoop out the seeds, putting
seeds into a small sieve set over a bowl.
Drain onion and transfer to a blender with coriander roots,
garlic, smoked paprika, salt and extra virgin olive oil.
Squeeze the excess water out of the soaked bread and add bread
to the blender. Blend until smooth.
Add red pepper and sherry vinegar and blend again until
smooth.
Add the cucumber and tomatoes and process until very smooth.
Stir in tomato water from the drained seeds.
Chill the gazpacho for several hours and then check seasoning—
it may need a little more salt or vinegar.
45 mins before serving, put the gazpacho in the freezer; leave
until it's forming icy shards around the sides of the bowl.
Meanwhile, make the croutons. Heat the olive oil in a small pan
over medium heat. Once oil is hot, add cubes of bread and fry,
turning often, until golden. Remove with a slotted spoon and
drain briefly on paper towels. Sprinkle with sea salt.
Cut avocado in half, removing the skin, and cut into small dice.
Serve chilled soup with croutons, diced avocado, chopped
coriander and lime or lemon wedges.

Lemon Sour Cream Cake

Ingredients
250 g (8 oz) butter
2 tsp grated lemon rind
200 g (7 oz) castor sugar
6 eggs
300 g (10 oz) plain flour
40 g (1.5 oz) self-raising flour
200 ml (7 fl oz) carton sour cream
Icing sugar to serve

Method
Grease a deep 27 cm (10.5") round cake pan, line base with paper, grease paper.
Cream butter, rind and sugar in a large bowl with electric mixer until light and fluffy.
Beat in eggs one at a time until combined.
Stir in half the sifted flours with half the sour cream, then stir in remaining flours and cream and stir until smooth.
Spread mixture into prepared pan.
Bake in moderately slow oven 160-180°C (320-350°F) for approximately 1.5 hours.

Leave to stand for five minutes before turning onto a wire rack to cool.

Dust with icing sugar before serving.

This cake will keep for one week, if you manage not to eat it before then.

Lentil Salad with Red Onion, Sun-Dried Tomatoes, Feta and Cherry Tomatoes

Ingredients
1 red onion, chopped
1 tbsp olive oil
1 garlic clove, chopped
200 g (7 oz) Puy lentils, rinsed
Hot vegetable stock, enough to cover the lentils
Handful of feta, cubed
Handful of sun-dried tomatoes, chopped
4-6 cherry tomatoes, quartered
1 tbsp each of fresh basil and mint, chopped
A little grated lemon zest
Pepper to taste. No salt needed as feta is already salty.
A squeeze of lemon juice
Extra virgin olive oil to serve

Method
In a pan, soften the red onion in the olive oil. Add the garlic clove and fry for 1 minute.
Add the Puy lentils, cover with the hot vegetable stock, bring to the boil and simmer until tender.

Drain and cool then stir in the feta, sun-dried tomatoes, cherry tomatoes, basil, mint and the lemon zest.
Season, add the lemon juice and drizzle with extra virgin olive oil to serve.

Classic Lemon Tart

My friend Denise Marchant gave me this recipe.

Pastry
150 g (5 oz) plain flour
40 g (1.5 oz) icing sugar
90 g (3 oz) butter, chopped
1 egg, separated

Filling
4 eggs
1 tbsp grated lemon rind
180 ml (6 fl oz) lemon juice
165 g (5.5 oz) caster sugar
125 ml (4 fl oz) single (light) cream

Method
Blend flour, icing sugar and butter until combined.
Add the egg yolk and process until the ingredients just start to come together.
Knead the dough lightly on a floured surface until smooth.
Wrap in clingfilm and refrigerate for 30 minutes.

Grease a 24 cm (9.5") loose-based flan tin.

Roll pastry between 2 sheets of baking paper until large enough to fit tin. Ease pastry into tin, trim edge then place the tin on an oven tray and freeze for 15 minutes.

Meanwhile preheat oven to180°C (350°F). Blind bake (lay baking paper over the pastry in the tin, fill with rice or baking beads) for 15 minutes, then remove the baking paper and rice or beads and bake for a further 5-10 minutes till lightly browned. To prevent over-browning, you can protect the edges with foil. Reduce oven temperature to 150°C (300°F).

Whisk eggs, egg white, rind, juice, sugar and cream in a bowl. Strain the filling through a fine sieve into the pastry case and bake for about 25 minutes or till set. Refrigerate.

Before serving, dust with icing sugar.

Raw Energy Salad

This is another version of the Grated Raw Beetroot and Carrot salad in *My French Platter* and was given to me by Jo Williams of Madame JoJos in Auckland. It's healthy and absolutely delicious. Eat it on its own or as a side salad.

Ingredients
¼ cup (35 g or a good oz) pumpkin seeds
¼ cup (35 g or a good oz) sunflower seeds
1-2 tsp cumin seeds
¼ red cabbage, finely shredded
½ red capsicum, finely sliced
1 large carrot, grated
½ red onion, finely sliced
1 beetroot, peeled and grated
1 cup (200 g or 7 oz) cooked quinoa, pearl barley or brown rice
1 tbsp finely chopped mint
2 tsp pomegranate molasses
Juice and finely grated rind of ½ orange
2 tbsp extra virgin olive oil
Sea salt and freshly ground black pepper to taste

Method

Combine the pumpkin seeds, sunflower seeds and cumin seeds and lightly toast in a frying pan over a medium heat, stirring continuously.

Combine seeds with cabbage, capsicum, carrot, onion, beetroot and quinoa.

Combine mint, pomegranate molasses, orange rind and juice, olive oil and salt and freshly ground black pepper. Drizzle over salad and serve.

Chocolate Brownie

Ingredients

250 g (8 oz) butter
430 g (14 oz) caster sugar
4 eggs
225 g (7.5 oz) plain flour
80 g (scant 3 oz) cocoa powder
1 tsp vanilla essence
Extra cocoa powder to dust

Method

Preheat oven to 180°C (350°F). Line a 20 x 30 cm (8" x 12")
slab pan with non-stick baking paper.
Melt the butter in a saucepan over medium heat.
Remove from heat and stir in the sugar.
Add the eggs one at a time and stir until mixture is thick and
glossy.
Sift the flour and cocoa powder over the egg mixture and stir
until well combined. Add the vanilla. Spread over the base of the
prepared pan.
Bake for 30 minutes or until a skewer inserted into the centre

comes out clean. Set aside in the pan to cool completely. Cut into pieces and dust with cocoa.

Layered Bean Chilli

Ingredients
2 large onions, chopped
1 large green pepper, seeded and chopped
3 tbsp salad oil
1 tbsp mustard seeds
1 tbsp chilli powder
1 tsp cumin seeds
1 tsp unsweetened cocoa
¼ tsp ground cinnamon
400 g (14 oz) tinned chopped tomatoes
900 g (2 lb) cooked kidney beans plus 350 ml (12 fl oz) cooking liquid or water
OR 3 x 400 g (14 oz) cans kidney beans, undrained, plus 235 ml (8 fl oz) water
180 g (6 oz) can tomato paste
Salt to taste
Bag of corn chips—as many chips as you prefer
Chopped parsley, fresh coriander (cilantro) and grated cheese to serve (if liked)

Method

In a large pot, cook onions and green pepper in oil over medium-high heat, stirring occasionally, until onions are golden and pepper is soft.

Add mustard seeds and cook, stirring for 1 minute.

Add chilli powder, cumin seeds, cocoa, cinnamon, tomatoes (break up with a spoon if necessary) and their liquid, beans and their liquid and tomato paste.

Reduce heat and simmer rapidly, uncovered, for about 40 minutes or until most of the liquid has cooked away and chilli is thickened. Stir frequently to prevent scorching.

Season with salt to taste (not necessary if using canned beans).

Place corn chips on a large platter and spoon chilli over just before serving. Top with chopped parsley, fresh coriander, grated cheese or anything that takes your fancy.

Serve with a large green salad.

Acknowledgements

A huge thank you to all my family and friends who supported us with our move to France, helping me through the rough times and enjoying the great times with us—you know who you are. Also, thank you to those who encouraged the writing of our story once we'd returned to New Zealand.

I wanted to write about all the lovely people we met but it would have become confusing to name so many and tell their stories. However, I would like to acknowledge here my heartfelt thanks to all those we met and spent time with and the many kindnesses shown to Steve and me. So thank you to Lynn Backhouse, Michelle Fitzsimons, Suzie and Peter West, Guy and (the late) Erica Nicholls, Phillipe Camalet, Massimo and Jo Nebbia, Wendy and Colin Moger, Irene Stevenson, Jeanne and David Boden. Forgive me if I've omitted your name; it's due to my memory and not a lack of caring.